WOMEN
OF THE
DURHAM
COALFIELD
IN THE 19th CENTURY

WOMEN
OF THE
DURHAM
COALFIELD
IN THE 19th CENTURY

HANNAH'S STORY

MARGARET HEDLEY

FOREWORD BY JOHN GRUNDY

The
History
Press

First published 2019

The History Press
The Mill, Brimscombe Port
Stroud, Gloucestershire, GL5 2QG
www.thehistorypress.co.uk

British Library Cataloguing in Publication Data.
A catalogue record for this book is available from the British Library.

ISBN 978 0 7509 8988 6

Typesetting and origination by The History Press
Printed in Great Britain

CONTENTS

FOREWORD

This book tells the story of Hannah Hall, Margaret Hedley's great-great-grandmother, who spent her whole life as the daughter, wife, mother and ultimately the grandmother of miners in the pit villages of south-east Durham.

Before I read the book, I thought I knew what sort of life Hannah might have led. I expected there to be hardship and loss, determination and endurance, because like everybody else interested in that area in those days I had heard the songs and seen the pictures of women silently coping and suffering, waiting for the bad news from the pit, struggling with the poverty, and I found all of those things in this book. It does contain a great deal of sadness and hardship but to be honest it contains a lot more than that because we see the world through Hannah's eyes and most of the stuff that I already knew about, the masculine world of work and the pit, happens off stage. The men go off on their shift and come back twelve hours later to have a bath, get fed and go to bed. This book's unique selling point is that it explores what happens when the men aren't there, what happens to the women …

And I'll tell you what – a lot happens. Houses have to be turned into homes, births have to be survived – or not, childhood ailments have to be survived – or not, teenagers have to be guided through their most difficult years, aged parents need looking after before they die – the whole family has to be guided and protected from the worst effects of the monstrous cruelty of the system. Chapels have got to be built and communities kept going. These are the things that the women do. They are amazing. Hannah's amazing; I found myself really liking and admiring her and I'm sure you will, too.

You'll like her for the way she deals with all of those things, but you'll also like her because she's different. She makes choices and does things that are completely and splendidly unexpected for a woman in those days. She takes her life in directions that you would not have thought possible for an uneducated working-class woman. She will make you rethink your ideas of what women's lives were like in Victorian times.

Hannah couldn't read or write and she left no written record, so Margaret has constructed a whole life for her out of the bits and pieces that are available. She has woven together information from the broader history of the Durham coalfield and the more detailed history of the small communities of south-east Durham where Hannah lived. She's used the official documents that pin down the key moments of Hannah's life, the parish registers and the records of birth, death and marriage, and she has included a few surviving photographs and mementoes alongside those memories and legends that have been kept alive in the family. Out of those things she has created a vivid portrait of one lovely and admirable woman, and she has turned an important spotlight onto the lives of all the women of the coalfield, that almost invisible 50 per cent of the population who struggled and fought and kept things going through that whole period of extraordinary change.

John Grundy
Writer and broadcaster

INTRODUCTION

Hannah was my great-great-grandmother. She was the daughter, mother and wife of County Durham coal miners, and she lived through a significant period in both labour history and women's history. She was born in the first half of a very grim century for the working classes, married in the middle of it and died one year after it ended.

Hannah was typical of her gender, status and generation in that she was illiterate all her life – therefore there is no written documentation left by her on which to build her story. Also, there is very little written evidence about her, so I have told her story through the unwitting testimony of masculine and mandatory government records, together with family memories passed down through the generations.

The life of a woman married to a coal miner was not easy. Her living conditions were poor, her husband spent long hours away from the home and when he was at home he often needed to sleep while the rest of the household needed to work, and all of these things impacted on the women. She was required to provide him with a hot meal when he went out to the pit, at any time of the day or night, and she was also required to provide him with a hot bath and a hot meal when he returned from his shift, again, at any time during the day or night. This was made more complicated if there was more than one miner in the household working on different shifts. The routine of seeing men in and out to work was carried out alongside other household chores of collecting water, baking bread, making meals, shopping, etc. It was a relentless round of drudgery requiring much more time commitment than the twelve-hour shifts worked by the men. The early starts and general comings and goings made it difficult to enjoy a stable and comfortable home life.

Miners were noted for moving house regularly just before a new Bond was due to be signed and the women were required to pack up their homes and leave behind their support network of friends, family and neighbours and start again in a new neighbourhood that could be near or far, depending on the husband's knowledge of what was available. There are many instances of families with numerous children, each child being born in a different place.

By looking at Hannah's life and placing her in among what was happening to the Durham coal-mining communities of the 1800s, I believe I will be able to show how these women lived their lives, the issues that affected them and the many myths that surrounded them. I will illustrate that these women were only considered important by their families as they do not appear to have had much importance attached to them by the many men writing historically of the lives of the Durham miners.

1

NEW BEGINNINGS

'Where's Thornley, Ma?' Hannah Hall, aged 14, asked her mother, Annie. The pair were sitting at a table set under the window in their colliery cottage at Hetton-le-Hole, County Durham. They were busy with needlework tasks; Annie was a seamstress and had overseen the development of her young daughter as a competent dressmaker.

'Thornley?' Annie repeated. 'Well, it's over Haswell way. Why do you want to know?'

'Well I heard me da telling you we were moving to Thornley and I don't want to go.'

'Oh, so where are you going then if the rest of the family move to Thornley? It's your da's job, and if he thinks we should move, then we have to go along with it and nobody will ask your opinion,' said Annie, not taking her eyes off the work in front of her.

'But I was born here in Hetton and my friends are here, and I'll never see them again if we move,' said a petulant Hannah.

'Well you've got one thing wrong lass, you weren't born in Hetton, you were born at Great Lumley and you moved here with us when you were only two.' Hannah was obviously shocked by this news.

'That's where me granda lives, I didn't know we used to live there. So why did we move here?'

'For the same reasons your da wants to move to Thornley, for a better job and a better house.'

Annie knew it was true that pitmen like Bill were always looking for a better job, better house, better opportunity. However, she also knew that conditions either at work or home never got any better, wherever they had lived. Both she and her husband, Bill Hall, had been born into coal mining families in the Durham coalfield, so she was used to hearing the grumbles of the miners and their wives. After all, she had been hearing them since she was a little girl growing near Chester-le-Street. She married Bill in 1819 at the church of St Mary and St Cuthbert in Chester-le-Street and Bill had worked in a range of pits around that area before and since their marriage. Their move in 1822 from Great Lumley was prompted by the opening of a new pit in Hetton.

Coal in the east Durham area had long been thought to be hidden below the magnesian limestone strata. The existing coal owners, who didn't want to go to the expense of investigating the area, talked confidently of how there was 'no coal under the limestone'. However, geological reports found that the land was rich in coal but because of its position it would be expensive to extract. Boring through the limestone would also result in excessive water, which would require specialised pumping equipment, and a large capital investment. With the benefit of access to private bankers and investors, land agent Arthur Mowbray, an ex-employee of Sir Henry Vane-Tempest, set about creating an independent venture known as The Hetton Coal Company. This led the way for more pits to be opened up in the previously land-locked south-east Durham area, but while the pits were productive, working conditions were difficult.

Coal miners had been exploited by the owners for generations, and all had heard stories passed down of those who got rich from the labours of the men who were poorly paid and housed. However, when they heard that it wasn't one of the major land-owners planning to open a pit on the previously unexplored area in Hetton, many were only too happy to become involved. Not only was it the first pit to be drilled through the limestone, Hetton was also the first deep pit in the world and the first to be financed by money raised by private investors. Bill Hall was one of those excited by the new prospect. Already a coal

Hetton pit.

hewer in the Lumley pit in 1822, he was prepared to move his family to Hetton to meet a new challenge for a different type of employer.

Coming from a mining family herself, Annie realised that she was required to support her husband and the decisions he made about his work and their lives. She may not relish the frequent moves of house, but she would never question Bill's decisions. It was her job to provide him with a happy and comfortable home to come back to after his work at the pit. The move to Thornley would take place in time for the new Bond year – which would be 1 April 1837. Annie dismissed Hannah's concerns. She knew that when Bill told Hannah they were moving, that would be that! Her daughter had a lot to learn if she felt her opinion would ever be taken into consideration, and it didn't matter how old she was. However, she couldn't help thinking that she wouldn't have dreamed of questioning her mother when she was Hannah's age.

Thomas Wood, one of the shareholders and a former accountant of the Hetton pit, had sold his shares for £324,000 to invest in a new venture and now owned and managed Thornley pit in East Durham, trading under the name of The Thornley Coal Company. Wood was a

Thornley pit.

controversial figure in the coal industry. He was very much against the vend and in his role at Hetton refused to be regulated by the system. Nevertheless, the men trusted him because of his background.

The vend was a system whereby the major coal owners formed a consortium and decided how much coal each of them should be allowed to sell. By adhering to these rules it meant that no single owner was going to sell more coal than the others and the market would be equally shared between them. This was a rule that Wood and the Hetton Coal Company did not support. They felt entitled to sell as much coal as they could extract, and this decision made them unpopular with the land-owning coal owners.

Thornley was another previously land-locked area but with the arrival of the railways the coal could now be transported to Hartlepool port via Castle Eden station for sale on the London Coal Exchange.

It appeared that there were a lot of people making the move from Hetton to Thornley in time for the new Bond. Many of Hannah's friends would be joining her and her family in the new colliery houses that had just been completed in Thornley. Her father had told her that they were

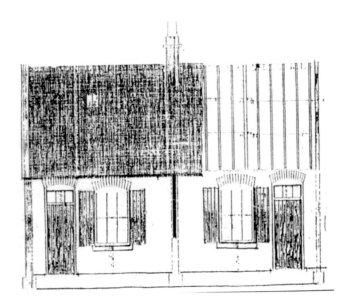

Plan of pit cottages.

exactly like the one they lived in in Francis Street, Hetton, so everything would stay the same – except they would be in a different place.

It was a bitterly cold day when the Halls arrived by hired cart from Hetton with all their worldly goods. The journey was an arduous one as the tracks were so narrow and rutted, and with the amount of heavy rain that had fallen the horse had difficulty pulling the cart. Their house was part of a long terrace in Second Cross Row and the same as all the other houses in the area. The homes were hastily erected, functional and close to the pit head. The coal owners begrudged any money spent on the miners but as the location had previously been only agricultural, with no available accommodation, it was necessary to provide housing for the workers who would ultimately make them even richer than they already were. The miners didn't pay any rent for the cottages and were considered 'very lucky' by the owners, to be housed for free.

Unlike the Hetton houses, which were built of brick, the houses at Thornley were built of locally available magnesian limestone, which was porous and made the houses very damp. The Thornley houses became noted for their smoking chimneys and damp walls. There is no doubt that the building material was chosen to cut costs and to further reduce the financial outlay. In common with the Francis Street houses, their new one had a ladder propped up against the loft hatch where they could gain access to the loft space. Once up there, however, the family realised that they couldn't use the space as there wasn't a ceiling and the roof was so badly installed that the room was virtually open to the elements. As this had been a feature of their house at Hetton, the Halls knew that their sleeping arrangements would remain the same – parents and younger children in the parlour, older children in the kitchen on fold-away beds.

A big black range in the kitchen would provide heat, hot water and cooking facilities, and once Annie got it sorted it would be black-leaded every week to keep it looking good as the centrepiece of any room should look. The room that housed the kitchen range was about 14ft square and had to serve as bedroom, kitchen, dining room, wash-house, hospital and mortuary. It was up to the skill of the miner's wife to make a cosy home and due to the training received from their mothers, and their experience as housewives, many were able to create and maintain comfortable and attractive interiors to their colliery cottages and provide homes of which they were proud. To an outsider, the colliery village was a dreary and dirty place but to the pit families it was what they expected.

The street outside the cottages was unmade and in the winter, such as on the day the Halls arrived, it was very muddy. There was no footpath and entry into the property was straight off the muddy front road. The muck heap was just forming when the family moved in. The method of disposing of household and human waste before a sewerage system was installed in colliery villages was to throw it into the space between two rows of houses, creating an open sewer. The manager of the pit sent men to clean up this mess periodically throughout the year. The muck heap, as it was known, was recognised as a place where diseases could spread, with illnesses such as diarrhoea sweeping through whole communities and killing the very weak.

At the back of the property was a small enclosed back yard laid with 'quarrel' – broken bricks, sunk in the mud to make a solid surface. There was a small shed that would act as a coal store. Many of the houses were empty but would become occupied quickly, and certainly before Bond day on 31 March.

Bill and his daughters, Hannah and Mary, helped the carter unload their belongings into the house. Annie stayed inside to get the fire going. She remained silent as she heard her husband shouting at the girls, 'watch what you're doing with that clock,' 'don't leave that chair out here in the clarts', and other comments that indicated his rising stress levels. He might be able to work in the awful conditions of the pit but Bill, in common with the other pitmen, couldn't cope with parenting; that was a job for the women. Eventually the fire was providing heat and their furniture and other items were at least in the house. Annie made the carter a cup of tea before he set out on his journey back to Hetton in the gathering dusk.

The next day Annie and the girls worked hard to make the dreary house into a home. The furniture possessed by many mining families, including the Halls, was often much better than the dwellings in which they lived. There was a distinct contrast between the external and internal appearance of the colliery houses during the 1840s. The proggy mats brought from Hetton were laid on the flag floor in the living room, the fireplace was black-leaded, and their brass fender set it off a treat. Ornaments were unloaded and set around the room. Their mahogany grandmother clock had pride of place on the kitchen wall and a much sought-after dess bed, also mahogany, placed against the back wall. The fold-away bed looked just like a cupboard by day but provided a bed for the girls at night. With the oil lamp on the table lit and with a cheery glow from the fire, this now looked a very desirable residence. Until, as the Halls found out later, once the fire and the lamp went out, the cockroaches came out to play. The colliery houses were noted for this infestation due to their dampness. The family had lived with this inconvenience in Hetton and learned that to keep them away they had to keep a candle burning throughout the night.

Bill went to sign on at the pit the next day. A colliery official read out the rate of pay and conditions available to those who had assembled. The Pitman's Bond stated that he was signing to be employed from

5 April 1837 to 4 April 1838. The Bond was a service agreement for each miner, what we would call a contract today. It was read out at the 'signing' by the viewer of the pit as most of the men couldn't read or write. Once the men heard the terms on offer, it was up to them whether or not they signed it. The first to sign received 10*s*, the second 7*s* 6*d*, the third 5*s* and all the rest 2*s* 6*d*. The men hated the system as they felt the Bond was unreasonable, it laid out rules about their working and living arrangements and it highlighted that the coal owner had control over all aspects of their lives. Any miner who broke the Bond was liable to arrest, trial and imprisonment. The information in the 1837–38 Bond was much the same as any other Bond and all favoured the coal owner.

Some 578 miners signed the Thornley Bond in 1837 with their cross, indicating their inability to write.

2

NEW ARRIVALS

Life in Thornley was much the same as life in Hetton for Hannah and her sister. As a dressmaker, the 15-year-old Hannah was sent out to farms for two weeks at a time. She stayed with the family and in preparation for her stay, the farmer's wife would have prepared a pile of tasks that she wanted completing. This could be mending, making or reshaping, all done by hand-sewing.

Hannah felt so grown up carrying out her needlework tasks; she was good at it and could make direct copies of clothes she had seen without making a pattern. She loved going to Sunderland with her mother to collect thread and other supplies from Mr Binns' haberdashery in High Street, and she always made a careful mental note of dresses on display in the window or on advertisements hung around the shop. Dressmaking was deemed more important than cleaning or laundering in the colliery village, so Hannah would probably have felt proud of herself and her achievements. Her mother, Annie, was well known to farmer's wives in the Durham area and worked out a rota for Hannah to follow in the Thornley area and also around Hetton. Her mother continued to work at home in her seamstress role and was well regarded throughout the district for making quality clothing. Hannah's sister, Mary, only 7 at the time of the move to Thornley, was also receiving training as a dressmaker from her mother. This cottage industry must have set the Halls apart from their neighbours, as they were not totally reliant on pay from the pit as most families were.

Women were not encouraged to work outside the home but many did as it was necessary to eke out the family budget. They often took on seasonal work on farms, cleaning and laundering; anything that would bring money into the home. Many families took in a lodger to provide extra income, and while it was inconvenient to share their space with a stranger, the lodger's rent would be useful if the pit was laid off.

Shortly after their arrival in Thornley, the Halls were to witness the disruption and riots caused by two Chartist activists who visited the village with the intention of educating the men about the unfair treatment they received from the owners and offering a way in which to fight this oppression.

Chartism was a national protest movement that had particular strongholds in the north of England. The People's Charter called for six reforms to make the political system more democratic. They wanted the vote for every man aged 21 and older, a secret ballot in any election and no property qualification for Members of Parliament in order to allow constituencies to return a man of their choice, not because of how much land he owned. They wanted payment for members so working men could afford to stand for Parliament. The Chartists also demanded equal constituencies so that all areas were represented equally, and annual Parliamentary elections so bribery and intimidation would be kept to a minimum.

Chartism came about as a result of the Industrial Revolution. The Reform Bill of 1831–32 and the New Poor Law of 1834 had both been seen as a betrayal of the working classes. The Chartists had a strong message, but its delivery let the movement down. The leadership was strong but as this was a nationwide movement there weren't enough leaders to get the message around the country and the job of doing so was devolved to those with oratory skills. Unfortunately, the message was sometimes distorted and Chartists became known for their bullying and violent tactics, which in turn led to the downfall of the organisation.

The People's Charter was not enacted in the 1840s and in the short-term Chartism failed, but it was a movement founded on an optimism that was eventually justified. It was a powerful assertion of the rights of working people, creating in them a long-term self-confidence and self-reliance. However, the demands of the Charter weren't passed into law until long after the movement ended.

At a meeting in Thornley in March 1839, the Chartists enrolled sixty new members, a significant number being well-known Primitive Methodists. Methodism was very strong in Thornley as it was one of the most isolated mining communities. It offered miners the opportunity to attend classes, meetings, discussions and fund-raising activities. It also became a school for self-help. The chapel gave the miners some of their first experience of music, literature and philosophy, and was often their first social centre. They drew together at the chapel and found strength in their weaknesses.

Bill came home for his tea on the afternoon the Chartist agitators arrived and told Annie, 'I don't like the sound of those two men who call themselves Chartists. More like troublemakers to me. They're firing the lads up to strike by giving them an example of something that's happened in a pit in Northumberland, nothing to do with us.'

'Well if you think they're in the wrong, you don't have to strike, do you?' replied Annie, knowing full well that if the rest of the pit went out on strike then so would he.

'We've got to stick together, you know that,' Bill said. 'Some of the younger lads just see it as a bit of excitement, but you know what powers the owners have if we upset them. The first thing they'll do is turn us out of our homes, and that wouldn't be very pleasant the way the weather is at the moment.' They both fell silent to ponder their thoughts.

The Chartists were still in the village at the end of August. Thornley was known as a militant area and the support the Chartists received was among the best in the country. Special constables were stationed in and around the village to try and stop any trouble and they accompanied the dwindling number of workers prepared to go to the pit. Whether it was fear of the Chartists' intimidation or a genuine desire to support their cause that kept men from their jobs is not known.

Bill told Annie, 'The lads are more frightened of them Chartists than they are of the owners, that's why they're staying away from the pit.'

Annie looked at him and thought, 'Yes, and you're one of them.'

Of course, she realised that it was difficult to go against your work-mates and as his wife, while she might not agree with his actions, Annie knew she had to support her husband. If she didn't support him, it would lead to trouble at home. Pitmen almost always married women from within the industry who understood the importance of standing together at times of unrest in the pit. The last thing a husband needed was his wife encouraging him to stand alone.

Bill had withdrawn his labour along with large numbers of Thornley miners as a result of intimidation from the Chartists and village men who had been converted by them. He realised that he was being bul-lied but was keen to be seen to be supporting his workmates. No man wanted to stand alone and the number still working was fewer every day. The Chartists and their Thornley converts committed violent acts to bring work at the pit to a halt, and while there is no evidence to sug-gest that Bill or his family were involved, there is no doubt they would have witnessed what was going on.

Thornley appeared in an article in *The Northern Liberator* concern-ing the strength of the women's Chartist group in Thornley. Annie knew of the group and had been asked to join but she wasn't going to get involved and urged Hannah, now aged 17, not to allow herself to be dragged in either. She thought the women should be fighting to improve their own circumstances, but they were fighting for better conditions and pay for their menfolk.

The women had baked a pie weighing over 3st in support of the cause. They held teas, fetes and socials to raise money for the Chartist movement and while there is no direct evidence to suggest Hannah was involved, it is clear from newspaper reports that all the village women were drawn into the debate. Annie knew that the men had difficult jobs in hazardous surroundings where they worked twelve-hour shifts, but she also knew that they had time off and she didn't know many women who had any time off from the drudgery of household chores. Around the time of the unrest, the village had a visit from Lady Pease, a leading female Chartist in the north of England and well known for supporting the cause of the working classes, but Annie didn't attend that meeting.

She knew that Lady Pease probably meant well but doubted if she had ever had the workload of a pitman's wife either.

Things came to a head one day when Bill's mates from the pit, Joe Smith, Jack Redfern, Joe Craig and Will Steel, were arrested as agitators. These were miners who had taken on the mantle of the Chartists and were bullying pitmen to stay away from work. The four were taken to Durham Magistrates' Court and committed to six weeks' hard labour on the treadmill. Bill was shocked and told Annie, 'Bloody fools. What will happen to their wives and bairns now that they're missing for six weeks. The owners will not let them stay in their pit houses. Is there only me can see through them Chartists?'

Annie said, 'They won't have given their families a second thought. There's no knowing how long they will be away, or if the owners will even let them return to the pit.'

When the other Thornley miners learned of the fate of their four colleagues they were shocked, and the incident appeared to make them look at the situation in a new way. An open-air meeting was called to discuss a way forward. One of the more moderate men pointed out that they had withdrawn their labour for something that two strangers had told them had happened in Northumberland. He said, 'You have no way of knowing for certain that it did happen and yet you've let them whip you up into a frenzy, withdrawing your labour, putting your livelihoods and homes in jeopardy on the say-so of two men you'd never met before, and this has resulted in four of our own being put in jail.'

The men were mostly silent, then a spokesman said, 'Aye, we've been bloody fools. What about if we apologise to the owners and tell them that and ask them to release our lads from hard-labour on the understanding that we all go back to work tomorrow?'

There was a general muttering in the crowd as the spokesman said, 'All those in favour?' A chorus of voices shouted 'Aye' with arms raised indicating their agreement.

The man who had made the speech said, 'Well, it might be too little, too late, you know how awkward the coal owners are. They like nothing better than making an example of a situation like this.'

Bill agreed. He wasn't sure that the owners would be sympathetic, they usually weren't. In his opinion, once you upset the owners they were prepared to make you suffer and were in a strong position to do so. Anyway, Mr Wood was informed of the turnaround and he allowed the miners to return to work the next day. Their four workmates were released and things slowly returned to normal in Thornley Colliery … for the time being.

By 1840, Thornley had many public houses mostly located along the main street – Hartlepool Street. The presence of these pubs provided a temptation for the miners, particularly on pay Friday when they could drink or gamble away their hard-earned pay, some not having any money to take home to their families at closing time. At about this time, a preacher passing through the village of Thornley remarked, 'Thornley is a place for notorious drunkenness amongst both sexes, sunk and degraded are the people of Thornley – they have not been favoured with the tee-total lifeboat.'

Bill wasn't a drinker. He encouraged his family to attend the chapel in Thornley, not that he went much himself, but he didn't hold with drinking away the family pay, and he had witnessed at first hand the hardships suffered by families who faced a fortnight of no money for food. It was a sad fact that any man going home without his fortnightly pay would be the last one to suffer the hardship of hunger. His wife, while she might be very angry at his actions, realised that he was still the breadwinner and would always make sure he ate first. The children would be her next priority and she would be last, going hungry if there was no food left. These selfless acts were expected of her as the manager of the home and never questioned by the erring husband.

In 1840 Hannah would be 19 years of age, attractive, proud of her achievements and, as a result of her dressmaking skills, able to make herself look smart in the clothes she made. One afternoon in July, when she and her mother were busy with their sewing and Mary was out on an errand, Hannah told Annie that she was going to have a bairn. Annie laid down her work and looked at Hannah in amazement. 'But I didn't know you had a lad,' she said. 'Well, you'll have to get married. You

Hartlepool Street, Thornley.

won't be the first and you won't be the last that's been expecting before she got married, and there's many a worse thing.'

'I won't be getting married though, Ma,' said Hannah.

'You won't be getting married? What do you mean? Of course you'll get married,' replied her mother.

'I don't want to get married,' said Hannah, 'and I won't say who the father is either so me da can't bully him into marrying me.'

'We'll see about that my girl, I think your da will find out,' Annie said, shocked at her daughter's bluntness. 'And if you don't get married you will end up in the workhouse because your da will put you out.'

'I won't go to the workhouse,' said Hannah. 'I'll move in with our Ralph and Jane at Sherburn Hill until I've had the bairn.' Hannah wasn't looking at her mother when she said this, but Annie could recognise the defiance in her voice and realised that she was repeating a well-rehearsed speech. She also wondered if Hannah had confided in her older brother, Ralph, and his wife, Jane.

Near to tears with shock and hurt, Annie turned back to her sewing, dreading Bill getting to know this news. She realised that her eldest daughter could be difficult, but this was the first time she had witnessed her being downright defiant and realised that Hannah wasn't going to give in. It was unheard of for working-class girls to refuse to tell their parents the identity of the man who had got her pregnant without marriage and then dictate where she was going to live. Why was Hannah being so secretive?

Family reputation was a vital working-class asset, particularly among the more 'respectable' members of the local coal mining community, which Bill and Annie Hall felt they were. There was little shame associated with a pregnancy before marriage, provided matrimony ensued fairly rapidly once it became known.

Parents such as Bill and Annie Hall fully believed that any matters to do with family planning were best left unsaid in the hope their girls would remain pure. However, as with Hannah and many more young women, this was unfortunately not the case. Also, it was not considered respectable to know about contraception methods and together with the myths surrounding menstruation and conception among the medical profession until the late 1840s, it is little wonder that Hannah, an illiterate girl from a working-class background with no sex education or guidance, became pregnant. Hannah's pregnancy warrants our curiosity, however, as it did not lead to marriage. Hannah's child, a daughter, was born in January 1841. The home birth was straightforward with the baby delivered by Annie and Mrs Moody, a Thornley woman experienced in delivering babies. It is unclear who the father was – the birth was registered by William Scott, a surgeon working in Thornley at the time, and he wrote the name 'Henry Winship' on the birth certificate. However, on the baby's baptism record at St Helen's Church, Kelloe, the identity of the father has been noted as 'not known'. This information was given to the vicar by Hannah on the day of the baptism. There was a young man called Henry Winship living in Thornley at the time of the baby's birth. He was the same age as Hannah, a miner, single, and his family had moved over to Thornley from Hetton as the Halls had, yet there is no clear evidence that he was the father. If he was, as stated by Dr Scott on the birth certificate, why didn't Hannah give his name to the vicar? Dr Scott could have put any name on the birth certificate because as no one in the Hall household could read they would be none the wiser.

St Helen's Church, Kelloe.

Hannah's child would be the first in the Hall family to require a birth certificate. From 1837 the state took responsibility for the registration of baptisms, marriages and deaths in England and Wales. None of the family could read and write and it wasn't considered to be important, particularly for girls, so when an event occurred, the details were held by a literate local person, who would pass it on to the travelling registrar when they next visited the village. The custodian of the information may have been William Scott. It is not known whether he entered details of a father onto baby Ann's birth certificate to make Hannah appear respectable.

Bill wasn't a violent man but talking to Hannah to find out the father's name got him nowhere, so he shouted at her. However, Hannah remained strong and silent. Bill then threatened her with the workhouse, but she still stood firm. He had asked the young lads at the pit in a jovial way who was walking out with Hannah, not wanting to let on about her pregnancy of course, but no one knew. She and her father went through a period of not speaking that put a strain on family life but eventually, when Bill could see his daughter wasn't going to give in, he got used to the idea and couldn't bring himself to turn her out of the family home to the workhouse. He told a relieved Annie, 'We are in a better position than most to offer support to her and the bairn, and I couldn't let her go to the workhouse. I'm bloody annoyed at her but she's my family and the bairn will take our name. I just wish I knew who did this to her.'

Annie was shocked at Bill's reaction. She had felt sure he would have put Hannah and the bairn out and had thought that she and Bill would have fallen out as a result. It is significant that Hannah's parents offered economic and emotional support at the time of her pregnancy, despite how much they were opposed to it.

Annie did wonder why Hannah was keeping silent about the father's identity. However, baby Ann stayed with her mother in her grandparents' home and was known until her marriage as Ann Hall.

3

NEW REGIME

During the early 1840s, the population of Thornley continued to grow as the pit expanded. Families were moving from all over the north to work at the new pit. The Halls knew several of these families, who had moved from Hetton.

Hannah was worried about her mother's health at this time. She felt that Annie always looked tired but when asked about it she would be dismissive. There was only Hannah and her sister, Mary, at home and they tried to take on as much of the needlework as they could and also the household chores. Luckily there was only Bill at the pit. He always worked the night shift, leaving the house at 10 p.m. and returning at 10 a.m. There was a hot meal to prepare for him going out and a hot bath and meal to get ready for him coming home, but once both of those things were out of the way he was in bed for the rest of the day, getting up at tea time, when he would have a walk down to his allotment to check his plants and hens before preparing for his shift at the pit again. This was the family routine.

The three women were kept busy throughout the day. They had washing to do on a Monday, ironing on a Tuesday and baking, shopping and making meals from scratch every day as well as baking bread. There was also constant fighting against the grime of living so near to the pit head. Annie was pleased that the lasses could go and collect water for

NO. 9. GORE HALL THORNLEY

Law, Thornley

Gore Hall Farm, Thornley.

her. In Thornley the water came from a well near Gore Hall Farm and it was quite a walk. Annie had a rain butt in the back yard to collect water for washing and bathing but for cooking she needed fresh water. The farmer at Gore Hall would deliver the water for a charge of one halfpenny a bucket but Annie felt that was daylight robbery.

Their cottage was always clean and tidy with a good fire in the grate. Coal was another perk of the job of a pitman and was delivered every four weeks. Annie insisted that the flag floor of the living room was red-ochred and that the walls were whitewashed; it was important that standards were maintained. The kitchen range was black-leaded on a Friday and the brasses cleaned. Mary was responsible for cleaning the front step and washing the outside paintwork on a Friday – preparation for the weekend being very important to this and other pit families.

Part of the Friday ritual was the cleaning of their mahogany grand-mother clock hung in pride of place on the kitchen wall, which was polished within an inch of its life. Their dining table, which was scrubbed white, was used for meals through the week, but on a Saturday night Annie always put a green chenille cloth on the table to make it look special for Sunday. These rituals were important to mining families, who liked to be seen as respectable by the rest of society. The pit didn't work on a Sunday, so that's when they could be all together. It was the only day that the family ate together, and while the rest of the family didn't have to go to work, the women worked just as hard preparing the dinner with the family under their feet in the kitchen. Annie and the girls would spend the morning preparing vegetables grown in Bill's allotment and roasting whatever meat was available at the butchers. The meal wouldn't be complete without a Yorkshire pudding and this was always served first with the gravy from the meat, as a starter, to fill up the diners so they wouldn't eat as much meat for their main course.

On this Sunday, Bill and Annie's son, Ralph, and his wife, Jane, were visiting and having their dinner with the family. Ralph had moved to Sherburn Hill when he married in 1840 and his parents didn't see much of him, but he occasionally made the trip to Thornley on a Sunday to keep in contact with them. Ralph was two years older than Hannah, having been born in 1819. Hannah hoped to have a quiet word with him about their mother and her obvious failing health. She wanted to catch him before he came into the kitchen because she knew he wouldn't be able to keep the shock off his face when he saw the deterioration in her appearance. However, there was no doubt that the prospect of Ralph's visit had cheered Annie up no end, as she bustled around the kitchen happily preparing the dinner.

At about 1 p.m. Hannah told Bill and Annie, 'I'm taking the bairn out for a bit fresh air before her dinner.'

'Why don't you wait 'til after dinner, then you might get her to sleep?'

'No, I'll go now,' said Hannah, hoping that she would meet Ralph and Jane on the road. She left the house with baby Ann and walked to the top of Second Cross Row. She crossed over the road and walked a little way down Hartlepool Street, past the pit, when she saw two figures come into view. It was Ralph and Jane. 'Oh, thank goodness for that, it's your uncle Ralph,' Hannah told her baby. Ralph waved his cap at his sister in recognition. They walked towards each other and Ralph, taking hold of Ann, said, 'By she's a bonny bairn, how are you both doing?' The two women greeted each other warmly.

Hannah told him that she and Ann were fine and said, 'I've come out here hoping to meet you before you got to the house to warn you not to look shocked when you see ma.'

'What's the matter with me ma like?' Ralph replied.

'Oh, she's not well and she won't rest when she's told. She won't see a doctor, she's not eating properly, and she looks awful, but I don't want you to make it obvious because me da either hasn't noticed or he isn't saying anything.'

Ralph was quiet as they made their way back up the street, but the two women chatted away about the bairn, the weather and the journey from Sherburn Hill. Hannah liked Ralph's wife, she was about the same age as Hannah and as they neared the Halls' colliery house, Hannah reminded Ralph once again about appearing normal when he saw his mother.

'Look who I found outside,' said Hannah.

'Eeh our Ralph,' said Annie, grabbing hold of her first-born child. 'How long can you stay today? Hello Jane pet, how are you?'

'Just the usual Ma, I'm at work in the morning but I'm looking forward to your Yorkshire puddings, nobody makes them like you.' Ralph managed to look and sound normal. Hannah was relieved. However, Ralph was shocked at the sight of his mother. She seemed to have shrunk and aged twenty years since the last time he saw her. He was pleased to have had Hannah's warning before he reached the house.

'Come on then everybody, let's get round the table,' Annie ushered them all to their seats. All the chairs were different but there was somewhere for everyone to sit. Hannah and Mary plated the food up from the fireplace where it was cooking. Jane helped pass the plates around the diners. They had the best blue and white dinner plates out today and a matching jug for the gravy. Everyone was handed a Yorkshire pudding on a plate and invited to pour on gravy themselves. It was a very happy sight to see a family sitting down to their one dinner a week that they could share without work at the pit getting in the way.

Hannah looked across the table and was pleased to note that her mother was much more relaxed with her family around her. Once the dinner table was cleared and the table lamp replaced on the chenille cloth, Bill asked Ralph if he would like a walk down to his allotment. Ralph agreed, and the two men went out. Hannah put Ann down for a nap and the women, as they always did, got out whatever needlework task they were working on. Jane sat and watched them, chatting while they worked, pleased to be having some time off from her own chores.

'What do you think about your ma?' Bill asked Ralph as they walked down to the allotment.

'Aye, I got a shock when I saw her,' replied Ralph. 'Do you know what's wrong with her?'

'Well according to her, nowt,' said Bill. 'I've heard our Hannah asking her to see Dr Scott, but she won't. She just says, "I haven't got time for doctors, boil me some comfrey and let me drink the water." That's all she's taking.'

'Why, I don't think it's doing her any good,' said Ralph. 'Why don't you ask our Hannah what she thinks?'

'I'm not asking me daughter what's wrong with me wife. You don't do that sort of thing,' Bill replied.

'You do if you want to know the answer,' said Ralph, showing frustration at his father's attitude. The two men wandered around the allotment, not really taking notice of what was growing, and they eventually wandered back to the house without any decisions having been made.

Comfrey had long been used as a healing plant in Hannah's family. In the absence of regulated medication, the miners were early homeopaths and believed in the plant to stop heavy bleeding, relieve pain, treat bronchial problems, and heal wounds and broken bones. The plant was their first port of call at any sign of illness. They would make poultices for external wounds and turn the leaves into tea for internal ailments. They believed in the plant to promote healthy skin and general well-being, and it would be many years before research found that the plant may cause adverse health problems and should be used with care.

Dialogue about personal matters was not a feature of a marriage in working-class communities during the 1800s. Annie would never let on to Bill how she really felt, and he wouldn't ask. He would expect her to confide in a female family member, neighbour or friend, but would not expect her to confide in him about anything personal such as her illness. As far as he was concerned, he wouldn't confide in anyone – it wasn't manly, he would keep his worry buried inside him.

Just after Christmas 1842, Annie took to her bed. When Hannah got up one morning to start the chores, there was no sign of her mother and there was no fire in the grate. Hannah went into the parlour where Annie slept in the big bed with Bill. Annie looked as if she was still asleep. 'Are you all right, Ma?' Hannah asked.

'Aye lass, I'm fine, I just thought I'd have a bit of a lie-in today. Can you manage?' Hannah assured her mother that she and Mary could manage and left the room quietly. She told Mary to go and fetch Dr Scott.

'She'll not like it,' said Mary.

'I don't care, she can't go on like this. It's unheard of, me ma having a lie-in.' Hannah told Bill when he came in from work that the doctor had been sent for. He was shocked when Hannah told him that Annie had been in bed all day. 'She must be bad then,' said Bill. 'It's not like your ma to stay in bed. I'll go and sleep upstairs the day.'

The doctor arrived at dinner time. Hannah had taken her mother some tea and bread, but Annie hadn't eaten anything. She drank the tea but said she couldn't face the bread. Dr Scott went into the parlour to speak with Annie, while Hannah and Mary waited anxiously in the kitchen. When he came out of the parlour, the doctor said, 'Just let your mother lie in bed as long as she wants, she's very weak and mustn't have any pressure put on her. She's not well.'

Hannah pushed the money for his visit into the doctor's hand and thought, 'What a waste of money, I could have told him that.' She said to the doctor, 'Are you giving her a bottle?' He said, 'No, just try and get her to drink beef tea or some sort of broth at least twice a day.'

'Thanks doctor, we'll try. Do you want to see her again?'

'Not really,' said Dr Scott. 'Call me out if you think her situation changes.'

Hannah closed the door behind the doctor and went in to see her mother. Annie said, 'What did you send for the doctor for? What a waste of money.' Hannah agreed but didn't say anything.

'The doctor says you have to eat and drink regularly, Ma, to build your strength up.'

'I know, he told me, but what does he know?' Annie was clearly not impressed with Dr Scott or his advice.

Annie's situation deteriorated further during the early months of 1842. Hannah sent a note to Ralph and asked him to visit a bit more often and he and Jane managed to get to Thornley on most Sundays. The neighbours were helpful, for all they had their own troubles and workload, and could always be relied on to sit with Annie if she needed some company. Mr and Mrs Porter, neighbours from Hetton, had moved into Piggsford Street over the road from the Halls. They had been good friends of Bill and Annie when they lived at Hetton, and Mrs Porter came and sat with Annie most evenings while Hannah and Mary got on with trying to keep up to date with their dressmaking tasks.

During one of these visits when Hannah went into the parlour to take tea into her mother and Mrs Porter, she heard Annie saying, 'Well it's only to be expected you know, my mother died when she was young. She was only forty-one and I think I'm going the same way. I was only fourteen when me mother died.'

Mrs Porter said, 'Now come on Annie you can't think like that. Things were different then. They didn't have the medicine they've got now.'

'Well I've got the medicine that they had then − because that doctor was a waste of time − he didn't give me anything.' Hannah thought that her mother was right and was surprised that she would compare the situation between herself and her own mother. Hannah didn't realise that Annie's mother had died young and wondered if it was history repeating itself.

By the end of March Annie had deteriorated even further. Bill had been sleeping on a fold-up bed in the parlour so as not to disturb her and, while he didn't say much to his daughters, Hannah knew he was worried about Annie. Then, one morning when she went to check on her, Hannah realised Annie wasn't breathing. For all they had been expecting it, the family were shocked. Dr Scott was sent for and he confirmed the death and prepared a death certificate. The Hall family couldn't read what the doctor had stated as the cause of death but if they had they would have been shocked to see it read, 'general decay', in other words, Dr Scott had no idea why Annie had become ill or why she died − he put it down to general decay, an illness associated with old age. She was only 54 years old.

Annie's symptoms were most likely due to the menopause, a term probably not used in the colliery villages. The condition, better known as the 'change of life', will have been recognised amongst the miner's wives, and they would have been expected to put up with the symptoms. Women's health wasn't at the forefront of medical knowledge in the 1840s and it was a difficult concept for some doctors as a result of the lack of information available to them. However, Annie's symptoms of tiredness, lack of strength, loss of interest in food, etc., were typical of the condition and often described as a type of decay and a deficiency disease by members of the medical profession.

Annie was buried at St Helen's at Kelloe, about 4 miles from Thornley. All her close family were at the funeral. Ralph had the day off from his job and he and Jane walked over from Sherburn. It was a very sombre procession that made its way across the fields to Kelloe. There was a new church being built in Thornley, but it wasn't ready yet. The whole family were upset by Annie's death. She was an old woman at 54, no doubt due to her heavy workload, difficult pregnancies, poor nutrition and damp living conditions. Also, like most other miners' wives, she did not look after herself and always put the needs of others before her own. Hannah wiped a tear away as she watched the coffin being lowered into the ground.

Bill couldn't get over his wife's death. He was grumpy with his daughters and stayed out of the house at his allotment as much as he could. Hannah could have done with talking to him about the situation as she was missing her mother, too, but when she tried to broach the subject he stormed off, always having something else to do.

Mrs Porter from over the road was very good to the family; she would bring them a loaf she had made, or a cake. Her son, John, brought them over. Hannah had known John since their days in Hetton. He was about ten years older than her but hadn't married. He was a quiet man and always just delivered the goods sent by his mother and left. On one visit Hannah asked him if he would have a walk down to the allotment and have a word with her father. John was taken aback. 'What do you want me to talk about?' he asked.

'Well, his plants or the pit, anything really, it's just he doesn't talk to us in here and I'm worried about him.' Hannah could tell that John wasn't keen on doing as she asked, but he reluctantly agreed.

An hour later Bill came into the house with John. 'Put the kettle on lass, John and me will have a pot of tea.' Hannah was shocked at the change in her father. She looked at John for an explanation, but he just shrugged his shoulders. Hannah made the tea and put it on the table in front of the two men. Bill told Hannah, 'John says he'll help me down the allotment, I didn't know he liked gardening, and I could do with a hand. I'm not getting any younger.'

'Oh, that's good,' said Hannah, 'but you're not an old man, Da.'

'Aye I know that, but we should all be able to accept a bit of help when it's offered,' answered Bill. Hannah realised that he was thinking about Annie when he said this, but he was obviously feeling more cheerful than he had been for a while. She hoped her da was turning a corner.

John became a regular visitor to the Halls' home over the next few months. He helped Bill in the allotment and he and Hannah often had a chat. Hannah realised that she was depending on John for a social life. Even though she never went out of the house, she looked forward to his visits and he was good company. Hannah felt that her chances of getting married were very slim. She had a child and she had her father and younger sister to look after – what man in his right mind would take on anyone with that amount of baggage? She often didn't care, but there were times when it did get her down.

Hannah was shocked therefore when John suggested one day in February 1843 that they could do a lot worse than get married. 'Married to me you mean?' she said, shock written all over her face. 'Well, of course, married to you, who else would I be after marrying, your da?' They both laughed at this comment. Hannah said, 'Well we hardly know each other, and I have the bairn.'

He replied, 'Well we get on, don't we? And I like the bairn, I would treat her as my own. I'm a good worker, I've been on hewing for some time now, so I make good money and I don't drink or gamble.'

Hannah was overwhelmed. She had never thought that she would have the chance to get married, but she did like John and he was nice with the bairn. Her da wouldn't last forever and if she didn't take this chance now, she would be well and truly on her own. 'Well if you mean it, then, yes, I will marry you.'

John stepped forward and kissed her on the forehead. She put her arms around him and felt contented. She was also relieved that he hadn't asked who Ann's father was.

It is difficult to know if love was a deciding factor in working-class relationships when considering marriage. There were so many reasons to marry for convenience, as perhaps in the case of Hannah. While she was obviously fond of John, there is nothing to suggest that their relationship was built on love alone. She was not a good prospect due to her illegitimate daughter and elderly father and sister to look after. He was 33 years old and probably had a desire to father children. Another situation that often prompted marriage was when a young woman became widowed by losing her husband to an accident in the pit. There would be no accommodation made available for her and her children by the coal owners, so to keep a roof over their heads she would often agree to keep house for a widowed miner and eventually, in the name of respectability, they may have married. A third scenario may have occurred in a large family where, in order to free up space in the household, a daughter may be urged to marry. Whatever the reason in Hannah's case, the wedding plans went ahead.

The wedding took place in April 1843 at St Helen's Church, where the family had so recently buried Annie. Thornley church was almost finished but wasn't opening until August and Hannah and John were happy to be married in Kelloe. Hannah's father and John's father were pleased that there was going to be a wedding. Ralph joked, 'Well it's about time, we thought we'd never get rid of him.'

His stepmother said, 'He'll make you a lovely husband, Hannah lass. He's a good man.' Hannah didn't need their reassurances. She was sure that she was doing the right thing. What she didn't tell anyone, even John on the day of the wedding, was that she knew she was pregnant again and she knew that John was the father. She would wait a few weeks until after the wedding before she told anyone. She didn't want them thinking badly of her again.

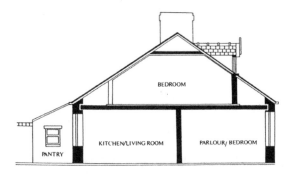

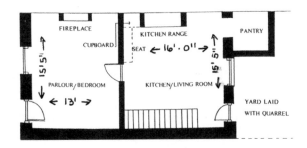

Interior plans of
colliery cottages.

The wedding took place on a Sunday and Hannah had made herself a
nice dress with bonnet to match. John wore a suit he had bought on a trip
to Sunderland and new bowler hat that he would probably only wear to
church occasions in the future. They made a handsome pair as they made
their way over the fields to Kelloe with their two witnesses, John's sister,
Mary, and his marra from the pit, Billy Cooper. Miners always married on
a Sunday as they didn't need to take any time off work. Parents usually
stayed at home and the happy couple would move into their new colliery
house after the wedding. In the case of John and Hannah, however, they
were moving in with Bill, Mary and Hannah's baby daughter. When they
arrived back at the cottage, Mary had made a cake and put out some
bread and cheese. John's father and stepmother had been invited and they
had a bit of a tea party. Everyone was happy that day. They had had their
sadness and now they could be happy about the future.

Bill offered to sleep in the attic space once the newlyweds moved
in. The space was very rarely used, but Hannah was pleased that her
father had offered as it would have been cramped in the two rooms
they shared downstairs.

4

STRIKING MINERS

Life got back to normal the next day as both men were back at work. Bill started at 10 p.m. on the Sunday night and John at 6 a.m. on the Monday morning. Hannah and Mary got on with their chores as usual. Monday was washing day and now they had another hot bath to prepare for a returning miner. John would come in from work at 6 p.m., when he would want a meal as well as a bath.

When John came home, everything was ready for him; his bath in front of the fire and his tea warming in the oven. Once his bath was over and he was seated with the family around the table he told Hannah of the death of a young boy in Thornley pit. 'Young Jimmy Barras, only eleven, was killed today. He was riding out on the shafts of one of his wagons and he fell off. Both loaded wagons drove over him. He didn't stand a chance, poor bairn.'

'Was it his own fault?' asked Hannah.

'Why, whether it was or it wasn't the owners will say it was. He shouldn't have been riding on the shafts, but they all do it,' said John.

'Me da always said working for Tommy Wood would be better than working for Lambton,' said Hannah.

'We all thought it would be, because Tommy was from mining stock – his father was a mining engineer mind, not one of us, but in some ways, it's a worse set-up than working for the Lord [Lambton]. Tommy borrowed money to start opening pits and he got others to borrow to invest in his pits and he has to see that they're paid their dues before anything else. The men aren't happy, and I think it'll get worse before it gets better.'

Hannah hoped John was wrong. She knew the pitmen wouldn't win if they went on strike, they never did. Her father had told her often enough of all the times the miners felt they had a good case, but it always came to nothing.

However, in October that year it wasn't just the miners of Thornley who were unhappy with their working conditions, a large number met at Gateshead to state their concerns at the conditions under which they were required to work. Some of their resentment was against the Bond, which they felt was harsh, controlling all parts of their lives. As a result of this meeting, the men from all over the Durham coalfield, including Thornley, came out on strike in November 1843.

'This is the worst thing they could have done,' said Hannah. 'Going out on strike in the winter. What if the owners put us out of our homes, where will we find shelter and live in this weather? I will struggle to survive under canvas at this time of the year and being so near my time.'

'It won't come to that,' said Bill. 'The lads are just making a point to the owners, they'll not evict us. They need as much coal as they can get during the winter.' He was to eat his words the next day, 23 November, when arrest warrants were issued against sixty-eight Thornley miners for not turning up to work. The men were taken to Castle Eden Magistrates' Court to answer the charge and said they would prefer to go to jail than work under the existing Bond. They were all jailed for six weeks. Their lawyer, Mr Roberts, had them released under a technicality, and all the men returned home, heroes of the hour. But the Bond remained. Despite slavery being abolished in 1833 throughout the British Empire, the Miners' Bond continued.

During the strike, in December 1843, Hannah gave birth to John's first child – a son she named Ralph after her brother and John's father. Once again, the birth was straightforward. Mrs Moody from the village came to help and Hannah was up and about in no time. John was delighted at having a son, 'and a brother for our Ann,' he said. This brought a tear to Hannah's eye, as John still hadn't asked who Ann's father was, but he was obviously happy to be her father.

In February 1844 news got around the village about a break-in at one of the miner's cottages. Bill came home from the pit one morning and told Hannah, 'Some men broke into Bob Wrangham's house last night while they were all in bed. They threatened to murder him if he went to his work at the pit.'

'Well who were they? Does anybody know?' asked Hannah, outraged.

'Well nobody's saying if they do and the talk is that there were others outside keeping watch so that them inside wouldn't be disturbed.'

'Oh, that's terrible,' said Hannah. 'What if they come here and did that to you and John?'

'Don't worry about that lass, they won't come bothering us,' said Bill, hoping that he sounded convincing. 'Anyway, the managers have offered a reward for information that will lead to a conviction of any of those involved.'

The people of Thornley were frightened but it wasn't the end of the trouble. It appeared that some in the village felt that the owners were getting off lightly by not addressing the men's complaints against the Bond. These men felt that if the Thornley men wouldn't come out on strike of their own accord, they would make them, like the Chartists had a few years earlier. Some nights later there was another incident involving intimidation, only this time a gun was fired at two houses in the streets where Hannah and her family lived. Again, the coal company offered a reward for information, but people were too frightened to come forward.

While they were having their meal one night, Hannah asked, 'Has there been any more trouble at the pit?'

'Well the lads are not happy,' said Bill, 'and they think now is a good time to make their feelings known, before they sign the Bond for 1844–45 at the end of March. They think the owners will agree to change to get us signed on for another year. There's going to be a big meeting of all the owners in Newcastle at the weekend and we'll send representatives to put our case.'

'I bet we don't get anything,' said John. 'They know we're desperate for the money they pay us and the roof over our heads. They even think we're luckier than some workers, them that live in the towns, for instance. We don't have overcrowding on the same scale that they do, and the owners know that that's our alternative.'

'Well, we'll have to wait and see,' said Hannah. 'We might all get a surprise.'

'I don't think I will,' said her husband.

News of the owners' meeting in Newcastle filtered through to Thornley during the following week. There was to be no increase in wages and they were to lose their guaranteed weekly wage into the bargain. This opened the floodgates for the owners to lay the pit off for a couple of days a week, therefore cutting overheads such as wages. This would make household budgeting almost impossible to plan. At least when the wages were guaranteed, the women knew how much they had to work with and how much they could expect in the fortnightly pay packet. Under the new scheme, it depended on how many days the owners laid the men off as to how much pay they would collect on pay day.

'Well I can't see anybody signing a new Bond after these decisions,' said John. 'Who in their right mind is going to work for worse conditions than they had before?'

'Aye, you're right lad,' said Bill, 'but it's not just Thornley that's affected this time, it's the whole county. There's going to be another meeting in Washington and I think we should go.'

John and Bill went to the meeting and the hundreds of assembled miners agreed they would not accept the new terms and they would stand by their demands by striking.

This was a blow to all mining families, but the Porters had more trouble. John's father, Ralph, died suddenly at the beginning of 1844. John was devastated. He had been really close to his father, staying at home longer than the rest of his siblings, working alongside his father in the pit and making an effort to like his stepmother, Dinah, when his brothers and sisters didn't. All of this was appreciated by Ralph. John also made sure that he got on with his half-brothers and sisters and so it was no surprise to Hannah that it was John, as a result of his maturity, who gave Dinah the support she needed at the time of her bereavement. The funeral was held in the new St Bartholomew's Church, Thornley, on 24 March. Ralph was 67. At least Dinah was

St Bartholomew's Church, Thornley.

able to stay in the colliery house as she had sons working at the pit.

Hannah was also worried about the strike. She was concerned in case she became pregnant again while the strike was on and money was short, but she had to put that worry to the back of her mind and concentrate on how to feed her family on less money. She and Mary still made some money from their dressmaking, but not as much as they had when their mother was alive because they had the household to see to. John and Bill would go out during the day and try and poach a rabbit or a hare and steal potatoes from the fields. Hannah did not agree with stealing but they had to eat, and Bill's hens had disappeared weeks ago. Some of the women from Second Cross Row were stealing coal from the heap and Hannah was tempted to go with them but when she heard that the police were waiting there to arrest anyone who went near, she changed her mind. The last thing her family needed was her being sent to prison.

In May, the Thornley owners brought in workers with no coal mining experience from Hartlepool to carry out the coal-winning duties of the striking miners. Despite having a police escort, these men were attacked on their way to the pit but once there carried out their duties to the satisfaction of the owners. The owners paid these outside workers handsomely for their efforts. They were determined to protect their new workers and a company of infantry was placed at Thornley Hall to deal with any trouble. The local miners were furious but helpless, and their families were starving. By the end of June, the owners implemented their ultimate deterrent; they began evicting families from their homes. Fourteen families were evicted in Thornley on the first day and the *Durham Advertiser* reported on evictions in every colliery village. 'We cannot even take them in,' said Hannah, 'or we'll be evicted. I hope they'll be all right.' Luckily the weather remained fine for outdoor living.

The owners were feeling no hardship from the strike. The pits were producing coal with their imported labour and by August the Thornley miners started drifting back to work, beaten by their own hunger and that of their families. At least four fatal accidents happened at Thornley pit during the strike period. These were due to lack of experience of the imported miners and a deterioration in the few safety measures in place. One incident was the breaking of a length of rope securing two workers during their descent, sending both men to the pit bottom. The verdict on their deaths was accidental death but they were no doubt due to the negligence of the owners in not making sure such crucial equipment was well maintained.

Eventually, at the end of 1844, the pits were almost back to normal with striking miners reluctantly returning to work having gained nothing from their months of hardship.

5

UPHEAVAL

Hannah worried about John and Bill's safety at the pit. She didn't want to lose either of them and the death of her mother and then her father-in-law had heightened her fear of death. If they were killed she would have to move out of their cottage and would be given two weeks to do so. This preyed on her mind as the number of fatalities in the local pits seemed to be getting worse.

Hannah asked John one night, 'Do you think there are more accidents since the strike? It seems that every day there's somebody else dead at the pit.'

'Aye, the safety checks were ignored during the strike and they've not been able to make the improvements needed quickly enough. Anything that costs any money is always ignored,' said John bitterly. 'When there's an inquest though, it's always accidental death – it's never the fault of the owner. I think this is the worst pit I've worked in, and that's saying something.'

'But they're all the same, I've heard me da say,' said Hannah.

'Aye, they are, but at least the Lord [Lambton] often had a fit of conscience over different things and he knew his workers. This lot wouldn't know you if they tripped over you, and they don't want to know you either. I remember an old pitman at Thornley, Neddy Rymmer they called him, he was a union activist and when he was talking about the

Thornley owners, he used to say, "I always thought, and still believe that the Lambton Collieries, on the whole, treated both man and beast in their employ with less severity than I found in other mining districts." I know a lot didn't have time for Neddy but I think I know what he was talking about.'

Hannah gave birth to her third child in 1846. They called her Sarah after John's mother, who died when he was only 4 years old. Throughout the rest of 1846 there was accident after accident at Thornley and the new pit at neighbouring Ludworth also owned by Thomas Wood. Many involved children, working in a dark and dangerous environment without adult supervision, and always the verdict at the inquest was 'accidental death'. Eventually, Bill, John and Hannah were all in agreement; the family must move on to try and avoid what John and Bill thought were negligent owners.

Talk of a move was put on the backburner, however, as family events took precedence. John's stepmother, Mrs Porter, asked Hannah one morning, 'Has your da been getting himself a new friend?'

'Friend?' replied Hannah. 'I don't know, do you mean at the pit?'

'Oh no lass, not at the pit – round Trafalgar Street.'

'Trafalgar Street? That's on the way to his allotment isn't it?' said Hannah.

'Aye, that's right lass. He's been spending a lot of time with Ellen McGregor down there.'

'Who's Ellen McGregor?' asked Hannah, the surprise showing on her face.

'Why she's a widow from Scotland who came to stay with relatives in Thornley when her man died. She has a bairn, he looks about fourteen or so. I think he's been set on at the pit.'

'And how old is Ellen McGregor?' asked Hannah.

'Well it's hard to tell, but I bet she'll be in her forties,' said Dinah. 'I've heard a few on about them.'

'On about them what?' Hannah almost shouted at Dinah.

'Well she goes down the allotment when Bill's down there and they walk back up Trafalgar Street together,' said Dinah.

'Oh, do they?' said Hannah. 'Well he hasn't said anything to me about it.' Hannah was annoyed that she had to find out about her da's 'friend' from somebody other than him. During the rest of the morning she couldn't get the thought out of her head and when he came in from work at 10 a.m., Hannah was ready for him. He had hardly got through the back door when she said, 'I hear you've got a new friend that you never thought to mention in this house?'

'A new friend? What do you mean? Let me get through the door.'

'I think you know what I mean, Da. Your new friend, Ellen McGregor from Trafalgar Street.'

'Oh, that new friend,' said Bill. 'Why I didn't want to bother you with it, she's just a lonely widow woman who happened to come down me allotment once or twice and we got chatting, that's all. I was lonely meself.'

'Oh, that's all is it?' said Hannah. 'And that's why half of Thornley's talking about it I suppose?'

'Get away with ye,' said Bill, raising his voice slightly. 'But I must take after me daughter if you think I'm good at keeping secrets.'

This hit home and Hannah knew at once what he meant.

'Eeh lass, I didn't want to keep anything from you, but I didn't know where things was heading at first. But you're right, I should have told you, especially since I think both me and Ellen feel that we've got a lot in common, and I'd like you and John and the bairns to meet her and her lad – Alex he's called.'

'Oh, right, so are you thinking of marrying her then, Da?' Hannah was shocked at her father's turnaround and didn't really know what to say.

'No, probably not lass, but I might put in for a house, and move her and the lad in with me, as my housekeeper.'

'*What?*' exploded Hannah. 'You might *what?*'

'Now lass, who cares whether we'd be married or not. Remember when you were having our Ann, you didn't care who knew you didn't have a husband and you know what, nobody did, and even if they did care, it was a nine-day wonder. No, we'll let folks think we're married and set up house here in Thornley. I think I'm too old to be married again. I'm coming up 60 you know.'

'Well, Da, I'm shocked,' said Hannah, but her father had taken the wind out of her sails by bringing up her out-of-wedlock pregnancy when she was only 20, and she realised that his support then meant that he expected her support now.

When John came in for his tea that night and Bill had gone to his 'allotment', Hannah relayed the conversation she had had with her father to her husband and Mary. 'Me da has a woman friend?' said Mary. 'Eeh I'm shocked.'

'Aye, he has, and he's going to move her and her son in with him in a colliery house.'

'And they're not getting married?'

'Apparently not,' said Hannah. 'He says he's too old to marry.'

'Well good luck to him,' said John. 'He's bound to be lonely and we are getting a bit crowded in here.'

Bill was as good as his word, and within a few weeks he had applied to the pit for a colliery house and been allocated one in Trafalgar Street. He then moved Ellen and Alex in with him. The rest of the village thought they'd been married but his family knew different. Ellen was introduced to the family. Ralph and his young family had come over from Sherburn Hill and they'd all had tea at Hannah's house. They agreed that Ellen was good for Bill and he looked younger since he'd set up in his new home. Hannah was happy for him.

During the tea party John brought up the much-discussed move to a Lambton pit but Bill told them he wasn't interested in moving now that his circumstances had changed. 'Well I think we'll be making the move,' said John, 'I can't work for an outfit like them at Thornley much longer, and I think we should think about moving to Sherburn Hill.' This was the most southerly of the Earl of Durham's pits and not that far away from Thornley. John was planning to move there in time for the signing of the new Bond.

Her father's bombshell was followed by another at the end of 1847, from Hannah's sister, Mary. She told the family she had a lad and if they were moving to Sherburn Hill, she wanted to stay in Thornley. 'Well that's fine Mary, you can stay in Thornley. You can go and live with me da and Ellen in Trafalgar Street. You're only seventeen, remember.'

'Yes, I know Hannah, but I don't want to go and live with me da, and Ed says we can get married if it would make things easier for me.'

'Get married?' said Hannah. Was there no end to the shocks her family were going to give her? 'Like I say Mary, you're only seventeen, and I take it it's young Ed Comby we're talking about?'

'Aye it is, and I can still get married if me da agrees, we can get a special licence.'

'Oh, so I see you've looked into this thoroughly,' said Hannah. 'Well it's me da's decision, not mine, you'd better ask him.'

'Aye I will,' said Mary. She stood up and walked towards the back door, lifted her shawl off the hook on the back of the door and left the cottage to go and visit her father.

For the third time in her life, Hannah's father surprised her by taking the actions she didn't expect him to take – the first time was during her own illegitimate pregnancy, the second when he decided to live with Ellen outside of marriage, and now he agreed to allow his 17-year-old daughter to marry by special licence. Hannah wondered how much his own situation had helped him decide on Mary's predicament, but of course, Mary wasn't pregnant.

Mary's marriage to Edward Comby was planned for February 1848 at St Bartholomew's. The Combys were a well-respected family in Thornley. Ed Comby's father, also Edward, worked at the pit with Bill and both decided that when young Ed got the chance of a job at Trimdon in time for the 1848 signings, that the young people should marry. The special licence stated that Mary was a 'minor' and that the witnesses to the marriage were David Adams and Dinah Ainslie.

At the end of March 1848 when the Bond at Thornley ended, the Porter family loaded all their worldly goods onto a hired cart and travelled to Number 220 Sherburn Hill – their new home – this time a two-up, two-down house belonging to Lord Lambton. It had the same appearance from the outside of all colliery housing, dreary and dismal and located within a stone's throw of the pit yard. However, once inside, it was immediately apparent that the house had been well cared for and with the help of 7-year-old Ann, Hannah scrubbed the house out while the furniture sat on the cart outside waiting to be brought in. Eventually beds were set up and furniture arranged, and by the time it came to light the lamps, it looked like home. Proggy mats gave a

Sherburn
Hill pit.

welcoming air and bedding and tablecloths were crisp and clean. The Porters' new home had all the hallmarks of a well-kept pit cottage.

John signed the Bond at Sherburn Hill pit and was in the same shift as he had been at Thornley. Life continued much as before for the Porter family, but more bad news was coming their way. One of Edward Comby's brothers knocked on Hannah's door on the evening of Saturday, 1 April 1848. John invited the lad in and they soon learned that Mary had been in an accident at her new home in Trimdon Colliery. While lighting the fire that morning, her clothes had somehow attracted the flame and she had suffered severe burns.

'I have to go to Trimdon,' said Hannah. 'Have you been to tell me da yet?' she asked the young lad. He hadn't, so whilst Hannah was getting her things together, John went off to hire the carter from Matty Robson at the Sherburn Hill Farm, to take them both, via Thornley, to Trimdon Colliery.

'I don't know when I'll be back,' Hannah told John. 'She doesn't know anybody in Trimdon as far as I know, so I'll have to stay with her.'

'Aye lass, you go. I'll get Jane to keep an eye on the bairns. She won't mind.'

Mary was so badly burned that there was nothing that could be done for her as she lay dying for two weeks, finally succumbing on Saturday, 15 April, exactly two weeks since the accident and only eight weeks since her marriage. Mary was just eighteen years old. Hannah nursed her sister throughout that fortnight, staying in Trimdon and unable to go home to see her husband and children.

St Mary Magdalene Church, Trimdon.

Mary was buried in the churchyard at St Mary Magdalene, Trimdon Village, on Tuesday, 18 April and the Durham Coroner's report appeared in the *Durham Chronicle* on the 21st, giving a verdict of 'accidentally burned'. Edward Comby must have been devastated. His new wife of only a few weeks, dead and buried. He remarried towards the end of 1849 in the church where his first wife was buried.

Hannah found out she was pregnant with her fourth child at the end of August in 1848.

Sherburn Hill pit, along with most others in the Durham coalfield, was on short-working at the end of 1848. The price of coal on the London market had dropped considerably and when the pits were on short-time, it meant that less was spent in the shops, so everyone suffered. The *Durham Advertiser* suggested that many men were being employed at a serious loss to the owners. It is just as well that no one in the Porter household could read that newspaper article. Short-working at the pit made household budgeting a nightmare. John and Hannah were lucky in that they still had money coming in from the dressmaking to help eke out their family budget. Before unionisation, the owners notoriously used the short-working system to cut their wages bills, which led to the hardship faced by mining families. They used any excuse to close the pit for a couple of days a week – geological problems, market problems, technical difficulties. All were excuses to lay the men off and therefore not pay them.

Hannah gave birth to a daughter in May 1849 and called her Mary Ann after her sister. Panic hit the area in the summer of 1849 when an outbreak of cholera was reported in neighbouring Ludworth. Recognising it as a killer, Hannah was terrified that her children might catch the disease. Sherburn Hill had a similar problem to Ludworth and Thornley in that human waste was thrown into the streets. The muck heaps were removed by the colliery company but not on a regular basis. There was no doubt in the minds of the families who lived in these conditions that it was where the cholera had come from. The muck heap in Ludworth was removed once cholera had been diagnosed and the place cleaned up. There was a slight outbreak in Sherburn and a team of men were sent there to clean up the filth to prevent a further outbreak.

'Twenty-three people have died in Ludworth of the cholera,' Hannah told John at the height of the epidemic. 'Revd Fitzpatrick from Shadforth has been to visit all the families who have lost someone to the illness, and I saw him in Sherburn this morning.'

'Aye he's a good man, the Reverend,' said John. 'But it will need a miracle to stop this disease once it takes hold in a place like this. No one seems to be bothered that we have nowhere to get rid of our waste and that's how the germs spread. When you put that with the poor quality of our water, it's no wonder folks die,' said John.

'The water comes from the pit though,' said Hannah.

'Aye but it's not perfect, God knows what's in it,' her husband replied. 'We might as well be drinking the water from the water butt in the yard. I heard from someone at the pit that even in Durham city they're trying to get rid of human waste into the river by building a big sewer. It will never happen here because the coal owners wouldn't pay for it and I bet their families are not affected by cholera.'

With the pit on short-working and Hannah never knowing how much John was going to be bringing in on the fortnightly pay Friday, she was becoming more and more dependent on the dressmaking money that she managed to earn. Late in 1849, her father asked if she could manage to look after a lodger as well as everything else. 'I knew his parents from Great Lumley,' Bill said. 'The lad can't get work there, but he's been set on at Sherburn as a blacksmith, and because he's single, there's nowhere for him to live. I said I would ask but told him you were full to the gunnels to start with.'

'Well I think it would be a good idea to take a lodger,' said Hannah. 'His money will make budgeting for a fortnight a lot easier than it is at present, but he'll have to sleep in the loft space.' So it was agreed, Matthew Addison was to move in with the Porters and sleep in the loft.

At the beginning of 1850, Hannah's daughter, Sarah, aged just 3½, and John Porter's eldest daughter became ill. It started off as a cold. Sarah couldn't keep warm and then she was too hot. Hannah found someone in the Sherburn Hill area with a comfrey plant and boiled the leaves, giving the water to Sarah to drink. She did seem to pick up for a while but then her condition deteriorated quickly. She was listless and pale, and Hannah could see that she had lost some weight. Her cough developed rapidly and was unrelenting, but when Sarah began coughing up blood Hannah knew it was very serious. Doctor Harrison was sent for and he gave advice – he probably realised that Sarah had consumption and that she was unlikely to recover, but he didn't tell Hannah that. He told Hannah that Sarah needed fresh air and plenty of full milk to drink. To save money, Hannah, like so many of the women in the colliery villages, only got half milk from the farmer when he made his deliveries. The farmer would measure out half a jug of milk, and Hannah would fill the jug up with the water she collected from the village tap. Now, however, she was in a position to get full milk when the farmer came round, as a result of the lodger's money, and she could still get the half milk for the rest of the family.

Sarah had no appetite, but drank the milk given to her by Hannah and sat outside on the step when it was warm enough, wrapped in her coat and scarf. However, by the middle of April, she had deteriorated significantly, and Dr Harrison was sent for once again. This time, he shook his head and told Hannah, 'I'm afraid there's nothing I can do.' Hannah was shocked.

'But she's only three, doctor, only a bairn.'

'And that's why this illness has taken a hold so quickly,' the doctor said. 'She can't fight it.'

Sarah died the next day. The doctor wrote out a death certificate and talked Hannah through what he had written. 'I've put the date, time and place of death on here, the bairn's name, what she died of – and I've put phthisis, it's an old name for consumption, and the name of the person registering the death – your name. Is that all right?'

'Aye Dr,' said Hannah, distraught.

As Doctor Harrison left he thought, 'Sarah Porter isn't the first and won't be the last child to die of this illness in the area, and is it any wonder seeing how they live? The house was clean, but it was damp, the bairn was drinking half milk until she became ill and the water quality is appalling.'

The doctor was right, Hannah was to lose another four children to this disease over the coming years.

While the death of a child placed a great emotional burden on a woman, a woman who also carried a huge burden of physical work, there was still no discussion between man and wife about the death of a child. Of course, John was devastated when he found that Sarah had died, but he and Hannah grieved separately. Hannah confided in her sister-in-law, Jane, and became more upset that she couldn't confide in her mother or her sister, Mary.

Hannah gave birth to another daughter, who she named Sarah, in 1852 and a son, William, in 1854. William lived only a year, dying in 1855 of the same illness as his sister, phthisis.

The news sweeping the village of Sherburn Hill in 1852 hit Hannah harder than most, although she didn't confide this to anyone. A young woman in her early 20s from the village living with her widowed father in Sherburn Hill had concealed a pregnancy and the night before she gave birth it appears her father suspected and confronted her with it. Of course, the young woman denied that she was pregnant, and her father said to her, 'Well if thou is, thou's on thee own.' That night she gave birth to the baby boy in her upstairs bedroom, while her father slept downstairs and was unaware that the birth had taken place. However, she became ill the next day and a female family member sent for a doctor. Eventually it was proved that she had had the baby and concealed its body. She was then accused of its murder. The baby had been born alive and doctors in court suggested he had either been drowned shortly after birth or died of strangulation from the umbilical cord. Many in Sherburn Hill were called to give evidence to the court – the vicar, the teacher and shopkeepers – and all said the young woman was a lovely girl from a lovely family. Close friends confirmed that they had suspected she may have been pregnant, but she hadn't confirmed it to them. There were signs in the house, however, that she had been preparing for a baby, as baby clothes were found in her bedroom. Eventually, as the medical evidence was so contradictory, the woman involved was acquitted and the village breathed a sigh of relief. Had she been convicted of child murder, she would have been hanged. This sad story brought back Hannah's own situation, ten years before, when she had been pregnant, and she thanked her lucky stars for the support she had received from her family. She shed a silent tear for the young woman and thought 'there but for the grace of God'.

Cholera returned to County Durham in 1853 and notices were posted in the city of Durham and in the colliery villages giving advice on how to deal with the illness. This was that every house be white-washed inside and out, and that hot lime used for this purpose was available from the colliery store. Houses should be ventilated, and good fires maintained within them. At the first symptom of a bowel complaint, medicine was to be obtained from a doctor.

Hannah was devastated by this news. Having recently lost her daughter, she was terrified that her children would be infected with cholera. A letter appeared in the *Durham Advertiser* submitted by Nicholas Oliver, the Officer for Health for the Durham area, informing readers that 'the public health of the region is in an extremely good state'. Mr Oliver may have believed his own propaganda, but it is just as well the readership didn't contain many from the colliery villages who lived with the appalling conditions on a daily basis.

6

NEW WORLD

After William's death in 1855 and the resulting sorrow felt by the family, John told Hannah that a representative from a new coal mine opening in Australia was staying in Sherburn Hill and trying to get men to go and work there – taking their families with them if they wanted. John felt it might be just what the family needed – a new start.

'Australia!' said Hannah. 'How long does it take to get to Australia?'

'A few months I should think,' said John, 'but I think we should go. There's a lot from Great Lumley already gone and a couple have come back with plenty of money and jewellery. We've lost two bairns here because of the life we live through no fault of our own. The work at the pit is dangerous and badly paid, we have no say how we do things and we are slaves to the coal owners. If we left to go to another country, you never know, it could be the making of us.'

'Where will we live?' Hannah asked.

'There'll be houses provided by the pit, like here, only it'll be a lot nicer – everything will be nicer when the sun shines. We've got bad memories here Hannah, memories that we'll never get away from. This could be a new start for us all and we've got nothing to keep us here.'

That night Hannah tossed and turned in bed. She knew what John meant about a better quality of life and she wanted to do the best for her children, but she knew that because of their ages, Ann (14) and

Ralph (12) would probably want to stay in England and she couldn't think of leaving them. Hannah felt it might be better for John to go on his own, get the lie of the land in Australia, and if he felt they could make a go of it, he could send for her and the children.

She told John this the next day when they were on their own. 'Well I would like us all to have the chance of a new life together,' said John, 'but if that's what you want, I'll go and see what it's like and what's on offer. If I like it, I'll send for you and the bairns. I'll see how to go about getting it sorted out the day.'

John knew that he had to get Hannah and the children some rented accommodation as she wouldn't be eligible for a colliery house once he left his job at Sherburn Hill pit. Hannah was well known to the farmers in the area because of her dressmaking as a young girl. She suggested they ask at Shadforth Hill House Farm, just outside of Sherburn Hill, if they would allow her and the children to live in one of the hind's cottages. In lieu of the rent she would do all the dressmaking tasks for the farm and she and the children would help in the fields when extra hands were needed. In addition, Mary Sanderson, the farmer's wife, asked if she would be willing to take on some cooking when the need arose. Hannah was more than willing, anxious to have a safe roof over the heads of her family while John was away.

On Saturday, 14 March 1856 John and thirteen other men from Sherburn Hill travelled to Liverpool, where they would catch the boat to Australia. Hannah and the bairns went to Sherburn Station to see them off. The colliery band and banner were there and everyone who could had turned out to bid them farewell. It was like a carnival. Hannah cried as she waved the train away. She had to stay strong, her family were depending on her now.

John's travelling expenses had been paid by the Australian coal company he had signed on with and if he did send for her and the bairns, he would have to send their fares, or, as they had talked about, Hannah could sell the furniture they had to help raise the money.

Paradise Row cottages were isolated. They belonged to Shadforth Hill House Farm and were situated between Shadforth and Ludworth, just off the main track between the two villages. There were four cot-

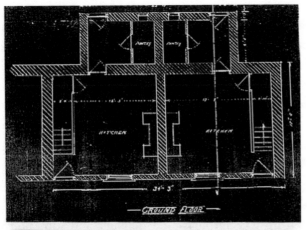

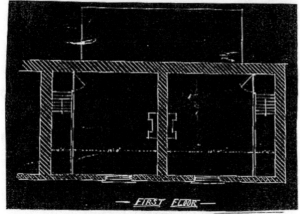

Floorplans of
two cottages in
Paradise Row,
Shadforth.

tages and Hannah was allocated number two. This house had one room
and a scullery downstairs and one room upstairs. Hannah and the girls
would sleep upstairs and son Ralph, now 13, would be downstairs.
Ralph was to work on the farm until his father returned and Hannah
was glad. She knew the lad wanted to go to the pit but if she could put
off the inevitable, she was more than willing to do so.

She already knew her neighbours. Neddy and Osyth Baldwin had
lived in Shadforth for about ten years, after moving to County Durham
from Norfolk. Neddy ran the Saddle Inn, a pub in Shadforth village,
when they first moved into the area and still carried out occasional
work there. He was also self-employed as a lime burner in the nearby
quarry as well as working for farmer John Sanderson at the farm. John

Porter knew Neddy very well from his days in the Saddle when John occasionally popped in for a pint and always spoke highly of him and his wife, who helped him out in the public house. The couple had four sons and a daughter, all of a similar age to Hannah's children, and it was nice that the children had company in their lonely location between the two villages.

The family were into a routine in their new home after a few days. However, on the Wednesday afternoon Neddy knocked on her door. 'Are you there Hannah?' he asked.

'Aye Neddy, what's the matter?' said Hannah.

'Well I've just been up to Sherburn on a delivery and somebody told me that all the lads that went to Liverpool on Saturday have been brought back.'

'Brought back? What for?' asked Hannah, puzzled. 'Who told you that? They wouldn't be coming back, they had a boat to catch to Australia.'

'Well that's what I've heard,' said Neddy. 'Nobody seemed to know any more details but the whole place is talking about it.'

'No,' said Hannah, 'it must be a mistake, nobody's been to tell me.'

'Well I hope you're right lass,' said Neddy. But Hannah wasn't right. The very next day John walked into the small kitchen of the cottage as Hannah was baking bread. 'Oh my God, what are you doing here?' she gasped, dropping the baking tin with the shock of seeing her husband, who she thought was hundreds of miles away.

'Lambton,' said John. 'We left the pit before the Bond period was up at the end of March and he sent the polis from Houghton to have us all arrested for breaching the Bond. There was about ten of them waiting for us in Liverpool.'

'Well the nasty buggers,' said Hannah.

'Hannah, watch your language in front of the bairn!' said John. 'But I know how you feel, I have been cursing him all the way back to Durham, and to think we moved from Thornley because we thought those coal owners weren't as good as the Lord. Well so much for our loyalty.'

John was crestfallen, and Hannah didn't want to make the situation any worse, so she busied herself with making tea, waiting for him to speak again. 'We had to appear before the magistrates at Houghton

Quarter Sessions. The annoying thing is that the agents of the Lambton pit didn't want to take the case any further – they were just making a point. Fred Sheldon and Bob Foster from Sherburn Hill agreed to act as bondsmen for us – £10 a man, to work at the pit until the Bond expires at the end of March.'

'But some of the lads will have sold all their furniture – them that was taking their families with them,' said Hannah. 'What's going to happen to them?'

'Why nobody cares about that lass. They'll get a cottage if they agree to go back to the pit, but they'll not get any furniture – they'll have to rely on friends, family and neighbours giving them bits to tide them over.'

'What about the money you paid over to the shipping company, have you lost that?'

'No, our deposits are in the hands of the ship owners, James Baines and Co. of the Black Ball Line. They've agreed to let us have our deposits back while we make our minds up about what we're going to do. Me and the rest of the lads are going to meet up tomorrow to decide what's next. Lambton's manager's told us that if we go back to our jobs at Sherburn Hill pit for the rest of the Bond period, then they'll release us to go to Australia.'

'Well, I suppose you could go to work until then,' said Hannah.

'Or just go straight back to Liverpool; we've got nothing to lose but I wouldn't put Fred and Bob's Bond money at risk,' said John.

'You'll have to see what the others say tomorrow then,' said Hannah.

The next day, Friday morning, John walked over the fields to Sherburn Hill to meet up with his fellow travellers. They had arranged to meet in the Lambton Arms. It was a sombre group that ordered their beer. 'So, let's decide what we're going to do, are we going back to the pit or back to Liverpool?' The group were divided. Many had lost their confidence and were aware that there was still twelve days left of the 1855–56 Bond to run. They were frightened that if they went back to Liverpool, Lord Lambton may have them arrested again. After more discussion, they all agreed that they would start back at Sherburn Hill pit on the following Monday.

'Aye we've lost again,' said John as he entered the kitchen. 'Back to the pit on Monday morning.'

'Well it's maybe for the best,' consoled Hannah.

'Yes, it might be,' said John, 'but I'll tell you something, as soon as that Bond's worked out I'm going to Australia as soon as I can sort it out. If this has taught me anything it's taught me what I already knew, that we don't have a life of our own. The owners have the last say in everything we do. And I won't be going to work for Lord Lambton on 1 April. I'll ask Jack Sanderson if I can work on the farm until I get something sorted with Australia.'

At the end of March, and the end of the Bond period, some of the men who had travelled with John to Liverpool decided to stay at the pit and went to the signing of the new Bond at the beginning of April. However, when they arrived at the pit head they were told that all those who left the pit and broke the Bond were to be placed on the county blacklist. This was the worst news the men could hear. Being on the blacklist meant that no other coal owner in the Durham coalfield would employ them for the foreseeable future. The men and their families wouldn't just be out of a job, but out of a home as well. This action by the coal company demonstrated once again how little the men were valued by the coal owners.

John worked for farmer Sanderson from April until October, when he managed to get a berth on a boat leaving Liverpool for Australia. There was no farewell party this time. John and Bob Aisbett were the only two leaving Sherburn Station on a cold and damp day in October 1856. Hannah had walked over to the station with John, leaving the children with her daughter, Ann. She waved until the train was out of sight. 'I wonder how long he'll be away this time,' she thought as she walked back to the farm.

As the weeks went on, Hannah realised she was pregnant again. She was 35 and worried about having more children because of those she had lost to phthisis. However, taking responsibility for the family on her own, Hannah didn't have time to think about her situation too much. As Christmas was coming, Mary, the farmer's wife, asked Hannah if she would help to cater for a get-together for the local hunt that was being held at the farm. Hannah wasn't a bad cook and Mrs Sanderson asked her to do 'sweet' while the 'savoury' would be cooked at the farm. Hannah decided she would do one of the three-tier jam tarts that her mother used to do for special occasions. She had plenty of home-made strawberry jam from fruit picked during the summer and quickly turned into a preserve. When Jack Sanderson came to collect Hannah's cooking, he was shocked at the elegance of the jam tart. 'Why that's marvellous,' he said to Hannah, 'it looks like it should be at a banquet, not just a meeting of the hunt. The wife asks will you come up tonight to help her serve the food?' Hannah was delighted to be asked. She would like nothing better than helping at the farm party.

Hannah arrived at the farm an hour before the guests were due and she and Mary laid the food out on the dining table. Hannah's three-tier jam tart was the centrepiece. 'Well I bet that gets some mention tonight,' said Mary.

'Me ma used to make them for special occasions,' said Hannah. 'She always said, "They don't cost a lot, but they look rich."'

'Well I think she was right,' said Mrs Sanderson, 'it looks lovely – was that your ma's cake stand?'

Mary was quite right, Hannah's jam tart was the talk of the party and she received many congratulations about it. 'We'll have to call you the queen of the tarts,' said Mary at the end of the night, 'and I'll certainly be asking for you to make that again.'

Hannah was delighted. 'Well it's simple enough,' she said modestly.

Hannah and her children continued to work on the farm – tattie picking in the autumn was back-breaking work, but their rent had to be paid, so it had to be done.

John and Hannah couldn't read or write, so it was impossible for them to keep in touch. John wouldn't reach Australia until at least April 1857 and then he would be sending her money through the post office at Shadforth. Hannah had told Mr Thursby, who ran the post office, of the arrangement and he said he would hold any correspondence that arrived for her until she called in. Hannah would be relying on Mr Thursby to read the correspondence for her, too. The post office was also the village shop and sold most things that the residents of an agricultural village would require.

The little family in Paradise Row continued in their routine without John and in July it was Hannah's time to deliver the baby she was carrying. Neddy and Osyth offered to take the two younger girls, Sarah and Mary Ann, to the Thornley Horticultural Show on Saturday, 18 July to give Hannah a rest. The two girls were looking forward to walking over to Thornley – they were aware that their family used to live there, but Mary Ann was only 2 when they left, and Sarah wasn't born. There was going to be a flower and produce competition, the Thornley string band would be there, cakes and cups of tea would be on sale, and if the weather was fine it would be a lovely day. George and Margaret, Neddy and Osyth's son and daughter, were also going to the show and they all left just after dinner time.

They hadn't been gone long when Hannah began to feel pains in her back. 'Oh no,' she thought, 'not today of all days, when Osyth's away.' She knew it was the baby coming. Her daughter, Ann, was the only one at home that day. Ralph had gone off with his friends and would probably go to the show in Thornley. Hannah waited as long as she dare, but this labour was progressing very quickly. Eventually she had to send Ann for Mrs Sanderson. 'Aw, Ma, I want to finish this shawl off,' complained Ann.

'Never mind that,' said Hannah, 'unless you want to deliver this bairn you're going to have to go for some help, now mak sharp.' Ann didn't need to be told twice. She ran out of the door and up to the farm to get some help for her mother. It wasn't long before Mary Sanderson and Ann were back, and Hannah had managed to get herself up to the bedroom. 'Get some water on to boil,' Mary told Ann, 'and have a look around for something to put this bairn in when it's born.'

It wasn't long before Ann heard a baby crying. She shouted up the stairs, 'Is everything alright?'

'Aye, it's a little lass,' shouted Mary, 'and she's a real bonny bairn.'

'Is me ma alright?' asked Ann.

'Aye I'm fine lass,' she heard Hannah say from the bedroom. 'You can bring me a cup of tea when Mary gets me cleaned up.'

Ann went upstairs with tea on a tray for the two women, wondering what on earth she would find, but everything was tidy. The bairn was in Hannah's big shopping basket wrapped up in her shawl and Hannah looked tired but happy. 'Well Ann, you're going to have to make the meals for a couple of days while your ma gets back on her feet,' said Mary.

'I can do that,' said Ann. 'Me ma has trained me how to run the house and I can do most things.'

When the two younger girls returned from the Thornley Show later that afternoon, they were shocked to find they had a new sister. 'What are we going to call her?' asked Mary Ann.

'Well I thought we might call her Susannah. Your da's grandma was called Susannah and he always said we should call one of the bairns after her.'

'Oh, that's a lovely name, Ma, she'll probably get Susan though.' Hannah agreed that they wouldn't give Susannah her full name, but she knew John would be pleased by her choice. She would have to try and let him know that he had a new daughter, born on the day of Thornley Show. Mr Thursby would know what to do.

Hannah made arrangements for Susannah to be baptised in St Cuthbert's Church in Shadforth. She would have liked to have waited until John came back from Australia but as she didn't know when that would be, felt it better to arrange the ceremony sooner rather than later. Hannah was a big follower of tradition and had been brought up to believe that after the birth of a baby, the mother and baby should stay in the room in which the baby had been born as much as possible before the baptism, as without being blessed in church, both may be in mortal danger. As this was likely to be inconvenient to Hannah, she arranged the baptism for three days after Susannah's birth, on 21 July. She was insistent on providing a christening bag. 'It's important to bring good luck to the bairn,' she told her children, 'and it's given to the first little lad we see on the way to the church.' The bag contained sugar (representing sweetness of life), salt (representing salt of the earth), candle (to light your way), spice cake or bread (so that you will never be hungry) and a silver coin (for good luck). If the

St Cuthbert's Church, Shadforth.

baby was a boy, then the christening bag would be given to the first little girl seen on the way to the church. Whilst Hannah's children felt this was most unnecessary, it was a tradition carried on by her family until at least the mid-1970s.

On 28 August Mary Ann and Sarah were excited to be going on a trip to the seaside. The Sunday school teachers at Shadforth were taking eighty children to Hartlepool. They were travelling on the train from Haswell, leaving at 7.30 a.m. Hannah was pleased that the girls were going on the trip as it would give her some time on her own. They were no trouble, but she wouldn't have been able to take them to the seaside yet, not with baby Susan only a few weeks old. The girls returned at 8.30 p.m. after having their tea and some games on the vicarage lawn in Shadforth. They couldn't stop talking about what they'd done and seen at Hartlepool but eventually both realised how tired they were and took themselves off to bed.

Hannah and her children continued to work for the farmer at Shadforth Hill House Farm. However, their employer changed when Jack Sanderson died suddenly in 1858. Neddy Baldwin called in to tell Hannah that Jack, aged 70, had died peacefully in bed the night before. Hannah quickly got Susan dressed and hurried up to the farm to see what she could do to help Mary. Over the next few weeks, Hannah seemed to spend more time at the farm than she did at home and fed her own children there at Mary's suggestion. The Porters only went home to sleep.

Mary was determined to keep the farm going. 'We have 291 acres to see to and our William and John want to keep working it and I'm going to support them,' said Mary. 'Anyway, we have two labourers, the farm is in good hands.' Hannah knew that one of the labourers was their Ralph and she wished he was a bit happier about working there. He kept going on about working at the pit but knew that part of the deal with the Sandersons was that his labours on the farm helped towards the rent of their cottage in Paradise. Hannah didn't know how long she could persuade him to stay at the farm. If he left, then she would be in trouble with the rent as she had less and less time to devote to her needlework tasks.

Shadforth had always been an agricultural village and never had a coal mine, although limestone quarrying went on around it. In contrast, the neighbouring village, Ludworth, had a coal mine opened by the same owners as Thornley. The two villages were chalk and cheese – Shadforth was pretty and clean and Ludworth, like all mining villages, looked dreary and grimy. Articles in the local press about Shadforth concentrated on village life and country pursuits, such as when the Revd Blenkinsopp shot a quail in January 1858, the press reported that it was unusual to see a quail in County Durham and particularly in January, while newspaper articles for Ludworth focussed on problems at the pit such as strikes, accidents and deaths. The only claim to fame that Ludworth had, apart from its coal pit, was Ludworth Tower, the derelict remains of a medieval manor house that stood just outside the village. The local children were convinced that there was a secret passage under the tower that led to Durham Cathedral, but it is unclear whether anyone had ever proved it. Neither village had a railway station

Ludworth Tower.

or a major road running through them – the villages seemed to be on the road to nowhere.

In April 1858 Hannah commissioned a photograph of herself and two of her daughters on a glass slide to send to John to show him what baby Susan looked like. The process had been available since 1839 but probably not in the mining communities as a result of the costs involved, so how Hannah became aware of such a process is not known. She, Susan and Sarah visited a photographic studio, which would have been situated in a town, and had an Ambrotype photograph taken and mounted in a case.

The resulting photograph is impressive. Hannah has obviously dressed up for the sitting. She is wearing a dark-coloured dress with a lace collar. She has a brooch at the neck of the dress and is wearing a crochet bonnet with flowers at her ears, fastened with a blue ribbon. Her dark hair is parted in the middle and tied back, probably in a bun at the nape of her neck. Daughter Sarah is wearing a blue dress with pink edging. She too is wearing a brooch. Her hairstyle is similar to her mother's and

Glass plate image of Hannah and her daughters, 1858.

is also parted in the middle and tied back. It is not clear what the baby was wearing from the photograph but her bonnet, with a frill around the brim and possibly bows at the ears, can be seen clearly.

The cost of photography had reduced since its early days in 1839 but it was still out of the reach of most working-class families. However, with John away and sending money home, three of her children working on the farm and her few dressmaking tasks, Hannah was perhaps a little better off than most. There seems to be no doubt that she was a skilled financial manager, and well able to afford the luxury of a photograph.

7

MORE CHANGES

In March 1859, some sad news reached the residents of Paradise Row. Dr Scott, the surgeon who had delivered Hannah's first child, Ann, was killed in an accident while riding in a carriage being driven by his servant from Haswell railway station to Thornley, where he lived. He was only 46 years old.

Hannah heard the news while she was shopping in Ludworth the day after the accident. There were many witnesses to the incident and one was in Hall's shop telling what he saw. 'I was standing at the bottom of Hartlepool Street, looking along towards Ludworth, when I saw the phaeton coming quickly along the track. As they got to me, something frightened the horse and it took fright, and dashed away at a furious pace. The driver was struggling with the reins but was eventually thrown from the vehicle, Dr Scott just had to sit there, he didn't have the reins in his hands, and he was thrown out and fell heavily on his head.'

'Oh, that must have been awful,' said one of the women listening in.

'Aye it was,' continued the witness. 'There were a few of us and we could see the doc was hurt so we carried him to his home in Waterloo Street.'

Hannah didn't know Dr Scott very well but she was saddened by the news of his death. His Thornley practice was the first since he qualified as a doctor, and he arrived there in 1839. After delivering Ann he had always had a soft spot for her. Hannah felt she should try and go to the church where he would be buried, not to go to the service but to pay her respects outside.

She found out that the funeral was to be at St Bartholomew's Church in Thornley and on the day itself the weather was awful. The wind was blowing a gale as Hannah made her way over the fields from Shadforth to Ludworth and along the line to Thornley. As she walked through the village of Thornley she noticed that nearly every dwelling house and public house had their blinds closed. The shops were closed and almost every business, except the pit of course, was suspended for the day. There were crowds outside the church when Hannah arrived, too many to go into the building and not one of them complaining about the weather. A great crowd of people followed the coffin to the grave-side and heard the funeral service read by Revd Shute, which moved many of the congregation to tears. After the burial, members of the Oddfellows Lodge passed the grave in single file and each cast a sprig of privet on the coffin. Hannah thought there wouldn't be many men in a colliery village like this who the whole community would grieve over. An appreciation of Dr Scott's many acts of kindness and private benevolences had brought so many out to pay their last respects.

As Hannah made her way back to Paradise Row she couldn't help but think about John in Australia. What if something happened to him whilst he was there, what would she do? Dr Scott was about the same age as John and look at what had happened to him. Hannah was still worrying over this when she reached home. Her next-door neighbour, Osyth, was in the yard when Hannah arrived at the cottage. 'What do you think about them two?' Osyth asked Hannah.

'What two would that be?' Hannah replied.

'Well your Ann and our Billy, that's who.'

'Why, what have they done?' asked Hannah, fearing the worst.

'Our Billy says they're going to be wed. Wed I ask you, at his age.'

'She's only eighteen,' said Hannah. 'You don't think she's going to have a bairn, do you?'

'Why there's no other reason that I can think of to be getting married so young,' said Osyth. 'I've told him he should at least wait until he's twenty-one, then the money he makes at the pit will be decent, but no, they've made their minds up – they're getting wed this year.'

'Oh, are they?' said Hannah. 'We'll see about that. Our Ann hasn't said a word to me, not one word. Wait 'til I see her.'

Both women went into their own cottages with their own thoughts. Hannah wondered why Ann hadn't said anything to her. She couldn't believe that her eldest daughter was probably in the same situation that she herself had been when she was pregnant with her, at about the same age as Ann was now. Hannah didn't like to think about that time when she had disappointed her parents and wouldn't even tell them who the father of her child was. Well at least they all knew if Ann was pregnant that Billy Baldwin was the father. Hannah liked Billy. He was a black-smith at the pit and a very hard worker. He was always pleasant to the younger bairns too, but he was only 20 – what had they been think-ing about? 'She won't be the first and she certainly won't be the last,' Hannah thought to herself. 'It's history repeating itself.'

Hannah got on with her household chores. It was Friday, so that meant preparation for the weekend – the stove to black lead, the brasses to clean, floors to wash. She was glad of the distraction that the work provided her on that particular Friday. She had bread to make and also a dinner to see to for them coming in from the farm, so she didn't have time for much thought as the afternoon wore on.

Her children started coming home at about 4.30 p.m. Ralph was first through the door. 'Ooh ma, what's for tea? I'm starving,' his usual words upon entering the house.

'It's broth and dumplings and as much bread as you can eat,' Hannah told him. 'Get your hands washed.' One by one the rest of the children arrived home, all cold and hungry. Eventually they were all sat round the kitchen table with bowls of broth in front of them. The room was silent as they ate. 'Is nobody going to tell me what they've been doing today?' said Hannah. 'In a minute, Ma, we're starving,' said Ralph.

'Well I'm going out after me tea, so I won't have time,' said Ann.

'Oh, and where do you think you're going?' asked Hannah.

'Just to Nellie's in the village, I said I'd pop along tonight to help her alter a dress her sister's given her.'

'Well she'll have to manage without you tonight because I want a word with you.'

'With me? What about?' said Ann.

'You'll find out when we've cleared the tea things away,' said Hannah.

The rest of the meal was eaten in silence – the young people around the table feeling Hannah's rage. After they'd finished, Hannah said, 'Right, Mary Ann, Sarah, take these dishes into the scullery and get them washed up. One of you wash and the other can dry. I'll bring a kettle of hot water in.'

'But what about our Ralph, what's he going to do?' said Mary Ann. 'He always gets off with washing the dishes.'

'Well he's going to be filling the coal buckets both down here and up at the farm, so if you want to swap places with him, then go ahead,' said Hannah.

'No, it's alright,' said Mary Ann, 'I'll wash the dishes.'

Once the younger children were out of the room, Hannah said to Ann, 'Well have you got something you'd like to tell me?'

'No, Ma, I don't think so,' said Ann.

'Oh, I'm surprised, I would have thought you would want your mother to know that you were getting married,' Hannah said.

Ann remained silent.

'Well, have you got something you'd like to tell me now?'

'Who told you?' said Ann quietly.

'Well who could have told me? Don't tell me the whole of Shadforth knows before me?'

'No, I didn't mean that – I meant was it Billy or his mother?'

'Well for your information, it was Osyth, but I want to know why it wasn't my own daughter?'

'I didn't know he'd told his mother. We said we'd wait a bit, but he tells her everything, I should have known. Sorry, Ma, you should have heard the news from me.'

'Well it's not a case of hearing it from you Ann, it's a case of Billy getting permission from me to marry you – you're only eighteen remember.'

'I know, Ma, but I'm having a bairn.'

'Well I guessed as much – how could you be so daft? You know what I went through when I had you – your granda nearly put me out. I've told you that time and again, so I can't believe you would do the very same thing.'

'But I love Billy and he loves me, so we didn't see the point in waiting – we thought, "Well we're going to be together anyway, so why wait?"'

'Yes,' said Hannah, 'that's what they all think. I'll have to have a word with Osyth to see what we're going to do.'

'Do about what, Ma?'

'Do about you two planning to get married when neither of you is of age,' said Hannah.

Hannah took the poker and tapped on the wall at the back of the fire – a signal she and Osyth had if one wanted the other. It wasn't long before Osyth came in. 'Oh, I see she's told you then,' said Osyth, seeing Ann sitting at the table with her head down.

'Aye she's told me,' said Hannah, 'and she knows I'm not pleased about it, but the way I see it is there's nothing any of us can do about it. Is he willing to marry her?'

'Oh aye, can't wait, says he loves her. Love – what do they know about love?'

There were many tears and many cups of tea drunk in Hannah's kitchen that night as the three women discussed the pregnancy and its implications.

It seemed the bairn was due towards the end of the year and that's why the two young people had been in a hurry to get married. Osyth went for Billy and when they returned Hannah said, 'Me and your ma have been talking and we think it would be best if you got married and we'll support you as best we can. We think you've been daft to get into this position but as I've said to our Ann, she won't be the first and she certainly won't be the last to get pregnant before marriage.'

'I'm a good worker Mrs Porter,' Billy was anxious to point out. 'I'll make sure her and the bairn get the best I can provide. I don't drink or gamble and I'm good with me money. I'll make her a good man.'

'Well let's hope so,' said Hannah, 'because if you don't lad, you'll have me to answer to.'

That Easter, Mrs Sanderson had given the children time off, as long as Ralph went in to do the milking each morning. As it was a rare occa-

Shadforth Dene.

sion that they were all together on a Saturday, Hannah and the children walked over to Shadforth Dene. Osyth Baldwin went with the family together with Ann and Billy and the rest of her children, and all had a good time enjoying their freedom without having to work. They took a picnic – some bread and cheese to eat while they were out. Despite the weather being poor during the first couple of weeks in April, by Easter weekend the whitethorn blossom was firmly in bloom and the family were convinced that spring had arrived and it was very warm on the day of their picnic.

The next day, the family attended the Easter service at St Cuthbert's Church, Shadforth. Hannah didn't insist on taking the children to church regularly except on Easter Sunday. They were luckier than some children as a result of Hannah's dressmaking skills, and they all had a Sunday best set of clothes.

Hannah took the opportunity of speaking with Ann on the walk back to the cottage. 'You should have a word with Reverend Blenkinsopp about getting married here.'

'I don't want to get married here,' replied Ann. 'We are going along to Gilesgate to get married at St Giles.'

'Whatever for?' asked Hannah, obviously shocked by this new development. 'This church is on the doorstep.'

'Well that's why we don't want to get married here,' said Ann. 'We don't want everybody talking about us.'

'And you think that by going three miles down the road people won't notice that you're married? I don't know where you get your daft ideas from Ann, I really don't.' Hannah walked away from her daughter before she said something that she might regret. She had to admit though that Ann was showing the same stubbornness that she herself had shown when she became pregnant in 1840. Ann knew that John Porter wasn't her real father but she had never shown any interest in knowing his identity, which Hannah was pleased about as she didn't want to tell her.

Being under age at the time of her forthcoming marriage, the vicar of St Giles needed to see Ann's birth certificate, which Hannah had safely tucked away. Neither Hannah, Ann nor Billy Baldwin could read, so Hannah willingly gave the certificate to them to take to their meeting with the vicar. When they returned and Billy had gone home, Ann said, 'The vicar says me da was called Henry.'

'Oh did he now, and how did he know that?'

'It said on my certificate. I told him I was Ann Hall and the vicar said my da must be Henry Hall then and that's what will go on the certificate when me and Billy get married.'

'Oh well that's alright then isn't it?' said Hannah.

'Yes, Ma, it's alright with me but is it alright with you? I know you still don't want to discuss my real da.'

'Well I'm happy with Henry Hall,' said Hannah. So Henry Hall it was that appeared on Ann Hall and William Baldwin's marriage certificate. Hannah was silently grateful to the vicar of St Giles for not introducing Henry Winship into the equation.

Ann and Hannah worked on a dress and bonnet to match for Ann's wedding day, which was to be on 3 September. Hannah left the side seams of the dress as long as she could as Ann was gaining weight with the baby she was carrying.

When the big day arrived, the happy couple walked along to Gilesgate with their witnesses and were married at the ancient church

St Giles Church, Gilesgate, Durham.

on the outskirts of Durham. Ann looked lovely in her dress and the matching shawl managed to hide the thickening of her waistline. The wedding was on a Saturday – it was the Saturday after pay Friday, which was every two weeks, and as the pit wasn't working the celebration could take place. Hannah and Osyth had laid on a tea party, including Hannah's famous three-tier jam tart, for the wedding group's return and everyone enjoyed the day. Hannah didn't agree with having alcohol in the house, so the men went off to the Saddle Inn at Shadforth after the happy couple left to settle into their colliery house in Ludworth, where Billy worked as colliery blacksmith.

'I'm pleased that's over,' said Hannah to Osyth as they were clearing up. 'It's been a long day and I'm tired.' This was a rare admission from Hannah.

'Aye, weddings are always long days,' said Osyth, 'but they've gone now so you can get tidied up and then put your feet up.'

8

SORROW, CELEBRATIONS AND DECISIONS

After preparations for the wedding were over and everyone got back to normal, the families at Paradise Row were preparing for the birth of their first grandchild. Hannah set her two young daughters, Mary Ann aged 11 and Sarah aged 7, knitting squares that she would stitch together to make a blanket for the baby. The girls were keen to learn and anxious to help their older sister with her baby. Both had good needle skills for children of their age, as Hannah was determined her children would be trained in the art of looking after every aspect of a home, and a husband.

She had trained the girls to get ready for the weekly washing on a Monday. Preparations started throughout the colliery villages on a Sunday night, when the children grated the soap ready for the wash. Sunday was also the day everyone changed their underwear and Mary Ann and Sarah unpicked all the buttons on the thick cotton garments and put them to one side ready to be sewed back on the following Tuesday. Not everyone did this, but Hannah knew that if the buttons got broken in the mangle then she would have to replace them, which she felt was an unnecessary expense when she could use the exercise of removing and reattaching them as valuable training for her daughters.

Ann went into labour on Monday, 24 October 1859. Hannah was sent for around lunchtime just as she was finishing the washing and she and Osyth set out for Ludworth, leaving little Susan with her sisters. Ann was in the parlour of the small colliery-owned house and Hannah went in to see how things were. Osyth stayed in the kitchen with Billy, who was pacing the floor. Osyth tried chatting to Billy but he wasn't having any of it. 'She keeps this little cottage lovely,' said Osyth, 'Everything's shining.' Billy kept pacing and didn't let on if he heard what his mother was saying.

It wasn't long before Hannah came back into the kitchen and indicated to Osyth that all was not well with the pregnancy. 'Nip out and ask Lizzie Hartley to pop down, will you? I'm not happy with the way things are.'

'What about the doctor?' said Osyth. 'Should we send for him?'

'Well you can,' said Hannah, 'but we need somebody here quickly and if he's not at home, there's no telling how long he'll be.'

'I'll send our Billy to Thornley to fetch him,' said Osyth, 'and I'll go and get Lizzie.'

'What's the matter? Why do we need the doctor?' said Billy, concern showing on his face.

'Just to be on the safe side lad, that's all,' said Hannah, hoping she was reassuring him.

Osyth and Billy left the cottage and Hannah returned to the parlour, where Ann was showing signs of distress as a result of the pain she was in. 'It'll be all right lass,' said Hannah, 'Osyth has gone for Lizzie Hartley and Billy's gone for the doctor.'

'Do you think I'm going to die, Ma?' said Ann.

'Why no, of course you're not,' said Hannah with more conviction than she felt. 'Stop talking and concentrate on trying to relax, I know it's hard, but tensing yourself up won't help.'

'Oh, Ma, stop this pain, will you? And stop talking.'

'Well I can't stop the pain lass, all I can do is try and distract you, that's why I'm talking. Do you think you might like a cup of tea?'

'No, I don't want any tea, I want this baby safely delivered!'

'I know lass, that's what we all want,' said Hannah. They heard the front door slam as Osyth and Lizzie Hartley came into the cottage. Lizzie was the 'nurse' in Ludworth that women turned to when they were having a baby as her fee was much cheaper than the doctor. 'How's things?' asked Lizzie.

'She's in too much pain for me,' said Hannah, 'and she's never mentioned pushing.'

'Aye, well let me have a look at her.' Lizzie went into the parlour where Ann lay, writhing around the bed now, red in the face. 'Do you feel like pushing yet hinny?' she asked.

'No, not yet Lizzie. I've just got the most awful pains in my belly.'

'Well don't worry, we'll see what can be done.' Lizzie quickly examined Ann and said, 'I think you've got a way to go yet lass; let's hope the pain eases as the bairn gets ready. I'll ask your ma to make us some tea with comfrey leaves, that'll help you to relax.'

'I don't think I could relax Lizzie, I'm in agony.'

'Well we'll make some anyway and see how you feel after it.'

Lizzie went into the kitchen and said to Hannah, 'I'm not happy about this, have you sent for the doctor?'

Osyth said, 'Aye, our Billy's gone to Thornley to fetch him.'

'Well let's hope he can get here and quick,' said Lizzie. 'Make some tea with the comfrey leaves will you Hannah? It might calm the lass down.' Hannah went into Ann's cupboard and brought out dried comfrey leaves and mixed them with a few tea leaves. She poured boiling water over them. After a few minutes she drained the liquid into a cup and took it through for Ann to drink. As Hannah entered the parlour, she heard Billy arrive with the doctor. 'Oh thank the Lord,' whispered Hannah to herself.

Dr Russell came straight into the parlour. 'Now Mrs Porter, what is that you're giving her?'

'A cup of comfrey tea doctor, I thought it might relax her.'

'An old wives' tale, if you ask me,' said Dr Russell, 'but I suppose you wanted to keep busy.' Hannah scowled in the direction of the doctor, but he was busy examining Ann. 'And how long have you been like this?' he asked Ann.

'About three hours doctor.'

'I'm not sure where the pain's coming from,' said Dr Russell, 'but it appears you have a long way to go before the bairn will be born.'

Hannah glared at the doctor and thought, 'Fancy him admitting he didn't know where the pain was coming from, I wish he'd kept his mouth shut.'

Ann drank her tea and whether it was that that relaxed her, or whether she was just exhausted, Hannah wasn't sure, but she did settle down. The doctor stayed in the room and showed no signs of leaving, and this also worried Hannah. From her limited experience of doctors, she found them always in a hurry to be away.

Eventually, at about four o'clock, Ann let out a shriek. Hannah and the doctor both hurried to the bed and Lizzie Hartley came into the parlour. 'Oh, I think the bairn's coming, Ma,' screamed Ann. The doctor lay Ann on her side and examined her under the blankets. 'Yes, I agree, it's time,' said Doctor Russell.

Billy, in the kitchen, was horrified by the screams and shouting coming out of the parlour. 'Is she going to be all right, Ma?' he asked Osyth.

'Of course, lad, this is what it's like for women having bairns, it's a painful affair.' Billy was unconvinced but after one blood-curdling scream, he heard the cry of a baby. 'She's done it, that sounds like the bairn, I'm going in.'

'No, you're not lad. You'll wait 'til the doctor and the others have things put straight and then they'll tell you when you can go in. Do you know if Ann had a box ready to put the bairn in?'

'Aye she has, I think it's in the parlour with her,' said Billy.

After what seemed like a long wait, the doctor came out of the parlour and said to Billy, 'I'm sorry lad, you'd better go in. The bairn didn't make it.'

'"Didn't make it" – what do you mean doctor?' said Osyth.

'It was a long and difficult labour and he was too weak. He died shortly after birth. I am sorry.'

Billy was silent. He stared at the doctor. 'You mean there is no bairn?'

'No, he died shortly after birth – he just wasn't strong enough.'

Billy walked to the parlour door, but he didn't go in. He went back into the kitchen and sat in his chair in front of the fire, staring at the flames.

Osyth went into the parlour. Ann was crying uncontrollably, Hannah was visibly upset, and Lizzie was busy doing what needed to be done with the bairn to prepare him for his burial. There should have been a christening, but there would be a funeral. 'We were calling him John,' she heard Ann say between sobs, 'after me da.'

'Aye that's nice lass,' said Osyth, not knowing what to say. Osyth walked over to where Lizzie was with the bairn and looked at him under his shawl. He had a red face and dark tufts of hair. He looked perfect. But he was dead. 'Will you see Mr Thubron about a coffin and Rev Blenkinsopp about the funeral ma?'

'Yes of course I will, but we don't need to worry about that for the minute.'

'Yes, we do ma, we do. He needs a proper send-off,' cried Ann. Hannah held Ann in her arms and shed a few quiet tears herself. They were unaware that Osyth had left the parlour and now returned with two cups of tea.

'Thanks lass,' said Hannah. 'Lizzie's laid the bairn out, we'll see about getting him buried as soon as possible.'

Baby John was buried on a cold October day in St Cuthbert's churchyard at Shadforth. Mainly family and a few neighbours attended the funeral.

The death of a child was commonplace in the colliery villages and they outnumbered the deaths of adults, but statistics didn't make the grief any easier to bear for the young parents. The process of child delivery was primitive, left to the fortunes of nature for the most part. It was said that more babies died than lived and more so in the lower classes. In the case of baby John, his death shortly after birth may have been due to an over-prolonged labour or an infection his mother was carrying at the time of his delivery. Whatever it was, however, there was no investigation. It was just another part of life that the people from the pit villages took for granted.

Over the coming weeks, Hannah tried to get Ann interested in Christmas preparations. She set her on to make a mistletoe for the window. Ann was very creative, like Hannah, and carried out the task mechanically, but without any enthusiasm. Hannah suggested she make one for her own house, but Ann didn't reply.

Hannah also tried to get Ann interested in decorating the Christmas cake that was in storage, having been baked in March and 'fed' with a bit of brandy now and again. 'Will you ice that cake for me Ann?'

'Christmas cake? Aw, Ma, that's the last thing on my mind.'

'Aye I know it is lass, but it pays to keep thinking about other things at a time like this.'

'Well I think I can manage to put some marzipan on it; it'll look nice with a bit of holly on the top.'

'Why of course it would – nice and simple, that's always the best way,' said Hannah, pleased at the first bit of enthusiasm she had seen from Ann since the death of her baby.

The Sunday before Advent, known as Stir-up Sunday, was the day to mix the Christmas pudding so that it could be well matured by Christmas Day. Hannah made sure each of her family was in the house when she started on the pudding. Each family member had to take it in turns to stir the pudding with a wooden spoon; Hannah had been told by her own mother that this was to honour the wooden crib of the Christ Child and stirring was to be done clockwise to ensure good luck! The two younger girls took this task very seriously. Ann gave the pudding a stir and so did Billy and Ralph, even Susan was given a turn on the spoon. Once the pudding was ready, Hannah covered it in a cloth and put it in a cool cupboard where it would stay until after church on Christmas Day.

The Porter children were very excited on Christmas Eve. The house had been cleaned from top to bottom and looked festive with holly displayed around the room; the big blazing fire gave a look of homeliness. 'I don't think I'll sleep tonight I'm that excited,' declared Sarah. 'I'll be hanging my Christmas stocking up and thinking of me da on the other side of the world. I wonder what Christmas is like where he is? He might be sitting in the sun on Christmas Day, that would be funny wouldn't it?'

'Right you two, get your stockings hung up and then let's have you off to bed. Take our Susan with you and put her in my bed. I have some baking to do for tomorrow.'

'Baking, at this time of night, Ma?' said Ralph.

'Yes baking, if we're having our Ann and Billy for their dinners they'll probably stay for their tea and our Ralph and Jane and the bairns will be coming at tea time and I thought I would invite next door in as well, so I'll start by making a few pies.'

Hannah got started on the preparation for her pies. She had bacon and eggs in the house as well as some pork for the Christmas dinner donated by Mrs Sanderson from the farm as a thank you to Hannah for the support she gave her. Hannah was planning on what to feed her guests on Christmas Day as she worked. As well as the pies she was making, there would be cold meat left over from the pork, together with the sage and onion stuffing. She hadn't had time to make pease pudding but had plenty of chutney and pickles preserved from the autumn and there was always cheese in the pantry. She decided to bake a couple of loaves of bread before she went to bed that Christmas Eve, just to make sure everyone was well fed.

Ralph helped Hannah fill the girls' Christmas stockings. Each had an apple and an orange in them and two chocolate coins that Hannah had bought from the shop in Shadforth. She put a penny in each stocking and some nuts. With the baking done and the kitchen tidy, Hannah said, 'Well that's that then, I'm away to me bed, are you turning in too?' Hannah asked Ralph, forgetting the kitchen was his bedroom.

'Aye, Ma, I think I will. Merry Christmas.'

'Merry Christmas to you as well lad, I'll see you in the morning.' Hannah took a candle holder and left the living room to go up to the room she shared with her three daughters, wondering on the way what Christmas would be like for John on the other side of the world.

The next morning Sarah and Mary Ann were up before it was light, excited to see what was in their Christmas stockings. They took Susan downstairs with them. 'Eeh, Ma, look what's in here – some money,' Sarah was delighted with her penny piece. 'Can we eat some of this chocolate now?'

'You can have a little bit now but keep the rest for later. Mary Ann, will you start some toast off when our Ralph gets the fire going?'

'Aye, Ma, I'll see to that and the tea,' said Mary Ann, happy to oblige as it was Christmas Day.

After their light breakfast, the family set off for the morning service at St Cuthbert's Church in Shadforth. The weather was quite warm when they began their journey on foot to the church, and they met plenty of other families heading there from Ludworth.

As she thought, the church was full, and everyone was wishing each other season's greetings. Revd Blenkinsopp welcomed them all and wished his congregation compliments of the season, too. One of the Sanderson lads from the farm read the lesson and the Porter family enjoyed joining in with the singing. When the service was over, Mary Sanderson caught Hannah and reminded her of the farm party the next day. Hannah told her that they were all looking forward to it. This would be the third year they had been included in the Sandersons' party for their workers and tenants. It was customary for employers to entertain their workers on Christmas Eve but Jack had preferred Boxing Day, and now he wasn't here Mary was keen to keep the tradition he started. They cleared out the big barn and decorated it with holly, mistletoe and ivy, and hung lanterns around it. A couple of men from Sherburn provided the entertainment; one played the fiddle and the other a squeeze-box and their music was perfect for the dancing. Mary laid on plenty of food and drink – it was a gesture of thanks for the work everyone did for them throughout the year.

Once back in Paradise Row after church, it was all hands to the pump to help with the Christmas meal. Ann and Billy arrived, and Ann started to peel potatoes. Hannah had the pork in the oven and the Christmas pudding simmering in a big pan of water on the fire. 'Do you have Yorkshire puddings at Christmas Mrs Porter?' asked Billy.

'We don't lad. Mr Porter preferred onion pudding, so that's what I'm doing today, but I can soon knock you up a Yorkshire pudding if you want one.'

'Oh no, I'll have what you're having, it's just that my granny never made Yorkshire puddings on Christmas Day and it used to annoy me da.'

'Well if you're sure – it wouldn't take a minute.' Hannah had the dough for the onion puddings ready for the oven and she would put them in about half an hour before the meat was due to be served. The smells in the little kitchen that Christmas morning were making everyone's mouths water.

'Ralph, if you ask me one more time what time the dinner will be ready, I'll cut yer lugs off and roast them with this joint of pork. Why don't you all go for a walk around the fields for half an hour so me and our Ann can finish this dinner off?'

'All right, Ma, but mind, don't you and our Ann start eating without us.'

'Get away with ye, and you girls mind you put your coats and hats on. The wind's got up since we came in from church. Put our Susan's coat on Mary Ann.'

Once the two men and the girls had left the kitchen, Hannah said to Ann, 'How are you feeling today lass? It's bound to be a hard day for you and Billy.'

'I'm alright ma. I think I'm coming round a bit. I've been thinking about it a lot lately. If our John had lived, he might have been in poor health and I wouldn't want that for a bairn. They all need the best start in life and if he wasn't up to it, then it was God's way of telling us, by taking him.'

'Why lass I'm pleased you've got a bit of peace at last. It's never easy, it doesn't matter how old they are. I lost our William and our Sarah as bairns and I thought I'd never get over it, but you do. It's a common enough saying, but life goes on and it takes your mind off what you've lost. You never forget, but you learn to live with it.'

Hannah was pleased she'd had this opportunity to speak to Ann about the loss of her first child. They continued with their dinner preparations as they chatted, but the conversation was over once the walkers burst back into the kitchen hungrier than ever after the fresh air they had taken in on their walk around the Hill House fields.

'Eeh, Mrs Porter that was a grand Christmas dinner,' said Billy Baldwin when they had eaten.

'You'd better not let your ma hear ye say that,' said Hannah.

'Oh no, me ma makes a good dinner an all, but I love your onion puddings. It's the first time I've seen the Christmas pudding on fire, too.'

'I like to have a bit of brandy in at Christmas, it comes in handy for the cake, the pudding and the brandy sauce,' said Hannah. 'I normally don't hold with alcohol in the house, but at Christmas I make an exception. Now come on lasses, let's get this lot washed up and tidied away before them next door come in for the afternoon.'

When Neddy, Osyth and their four grown-up children came round, closely followed by Ralph, Jane and their children, the small kitchen was packed. When it was tea time, everyone said how little they would be able to eat. However, once the food appeared, it didn't take long before the table was almost empty.

After tea the little party played parlour games, sang Christmas carols and ate more food, this time washed down by Hannah's home-made ginger beer. It was about 9 p.m. when Ann said, 'Come on Billy, we should be getting along home.'

'Aw lass, stay the night, our Ralph can go next door and sleep with their lads, and you two can sleep in the kitchen.'

'Well I'm going round there to sleep anyway,' said Ralph, 'so you two please yourselves.'

'No, Ma, we'd better be getting home. I don't want to be sleeping on the floor when I have a lovely feather bed at home.' The Baldwins, Ann and Billy and Ralph and Jane were all preparing to leave the party to go to their respective homes, and lots of 'thanks', 'see you in the morning' and 'lovely day' were shouted many times before Hannah and her family were left alone in the kitchen.

Once the girls had taken little Susan up to bed, Hannah was left with her thoughts. Surprisingly, it had been a good Christmas without John, but did she really want to be working on the land during another cold spell? Ralph was wanting to go and work at the pit and wasn't enjoying the farm work any longer. His mates in Ludworth were earning more money than he was, and Hannah knew he had itchy feet. She didn't think she and the girls could put as much time into the farm work that the Sandersons would expect in return for the rent. 'I think it might be time to move on,' said Hannah to herself as she prepared for bed.

9

MOVING ON AND MOVING BACK

Hannah walked into Shadforth during the first week of January 1859 to speak with Mr Thubron about Seldom Seen, a small cottage at the back of his joinery yard. Mr Thubron also ran the Plough Inn but it was in his capacity as property owner that Hannah wanted to see him. There were two, one-storey cottages, Seldom Seen and Never Seen, and Hannah had heard that Seldom was available for rent. If these cottages had been in the town, they would be described as being in 'yards,' but in a small village like Shadforth, it was unusual for accommodation to be out of sight. The accommodation was small, but Hannah felt they would be no worse off than they were in Paradise Row. 'Can you manage the rent?' asked Mr Thubron.

'Well I wouldn't be here if I didn't think I could,' replied Hannah.

'Aye, well you're on your own with the bairns and I just wanted to make sure.'

'You can be sure I wouldn't take you down Mr Thubron. My man might be thousands of miles away, but I can still pay my way.'

'Well I'm pleased to hear it, but there is a problem with Seldom.'

'A problem. What sort of problem?' asked Hannah, her heart sinking.

'Well a few years ago I made a four-poster bed for me and the wife and when I'd finished it, she wouldn't have it in the house. Seldom was empty at the time, so I put it in there and I don't want to get rid of it.'

'Well what will I do with it?' said Hannah.

'Use it as if it was your own – it's beautiful – proper mahogany and I had red velvet curtains made for the drapes and the steps up to it are covered in red mats.'

'So, do I get a rent reduction then?' asked Hannah. 'After all, I love sleeping in my own bed and will really miss my comfortable feather mattress. If you could reduce the rent to make up for the inconvenience of sleeping in a strange bed, I might be tempted.'

'Aye well, I suppose I could, but I know you'll love the bed,' said Mr Thubron.

'Well that remains to be seen,' said Hannah.

'Oh, all right I'll knock sixpence a week off the rent.'

'That sounds perfect Mr Thubron. I'm sure we'll be very happy in Seldom Seen. Now is there any chance of you helping to bring our bits of furniture along from Paradise Row?'

'You drive a hard bargain Mrs.'

The move took place that week, on 11 January, and Hannah felt it was the coldest day she had experienced in a good while. 'It's fit to freeze you,' she told Mary Ann and Sarah as they helped her pack up the family's belongings. Ralph was delighted that he was going to work at the pit. Osyth looked after little Susan while the packing went on and Hannah's daughter, Ann, came along from Ludworth to get things ready in Seldom Seen. One of the Baldwin lads was working for Mr Thubron and he brought the cart down to Paradise Row and the Porters goods and chattels were loaded on for the short journey back to Shadforth village. Osyth Baldwin took Hannah to one side to say, 'You've been good neighbours and you're now all part of our family so I know we won't lose touch. I'll be popping in to see you when I come to the shop.'

'And you'll be very welcome,' said Hannah. 'I've enjoyed living here, but I don't think I could cope with working in the fields any longer. It's hard work.'

'Aye I know lass, you can concentrate more on your sewing.'

When the cart arrived at the cottage, Ann came out and said, 'Eeh, Ma, what are you going to do with that bed?'

'Well I'm going to sleep in it,' said Hannah. 'That way I get sixpence off the rent.'

'I should think you'll all be able to sleep in it, it's that big,' said Ann. The children rushed into the cottage to look at the bed. 'Aw, Ma, it looks lovely,' said Sarah. 'It should be in a castle.'

'Yes, it's certainly too grand for in here,' agreed Hannah. 'Come on then the lot of you, let's get this cart unloaded and put straight before it gets dark.'

Hannah and the girls worked solidly setting up tables, chairs, unpacking crockery and linen until it was all done. 'I think it's time for a cup of tea,' said Hannah. 'Put the kettle on Ann.'

The fire had been lit early on when Ann first arrived and it didn't take long for the kettle to boil. 'I hope you'll be happy here, Ma,' she told her mother.

'Of course we will. We can concentrate on our sewing and our Ralph will get coal from the pit, so we can save a bit of money.'

Hannah and her family settled in well to life in the small cottage and enjoyed being part of a larger community once again. They still kept regular contact with Osyth and Neddy from Paradise Row and were shocked to hear from Osyth in April 1860 that Neddy had been declared bankrupt after the failure of his lime-burning business.

'I'm so ashamed,' said Osyth, near to tears. 'Our debts have just caught up with us, and there's something in the paper about it. Mary from the farm told Neddy.'

'Aw lass, I'm so sorry to hear that. You and Neddy are such hard workers. How can it happen?'

'Well, it's the customers who don't pay him and we still have our bills to pay. Neddy's so embarrassed by it all. He feels as if he's let us all down.'

'Oh don't worry lass, you've both got your health and your family. There's many a worse thing, and folks will soon forget. As for the paper, who do we know that reads one?'

There was a lot to keep them busy in Shadforth. The church was very active with socials and the girls loved going to the Sunday school. It seems there was always something going on. In July 1860, on the celebration of the Battle of the Boyne, members of the Orange Protestant

Shadforth village.

Association marched in procession from Sherburn Hill to the Shadforth church. They were accompanied by hundreds of supporters, bands and banners, and after the service they marched through the village. Hannah and the children were outside to see this rare spectacle, clapping and cheering along with everyone else.

There was no snow in 1861 until March but on the day the snow started, Mary Ann started coughing. Hannah was immediately concerned, remembering the deaths of her previous two children. She convinced herself that her daughter was just suffering from a cold, administered her a bowl of broth and ordered her to stay in the four-poster bed. She wrapped the oven shelf in a blanket and put it under the sheet on the bed next to Mary Ann. Hannah was so concerned about her daughter's health that she lit a fire in the small bedroom, to keep the girl warm. As always, Hannah had comfrey standing by to try and improve Mary Ann's symptoms.

Unfortunately, none of Hannah's ministrations worked and it was clear after a couple of days that the girl had contracted the same illness that had killed the other two children, phthisis. The doctor was sent for but was unable to offer any hope or help and Mary Ann died within four weeks of her first cough. Hannah was devastated. 'That's three of my bairns all dead of the same thing, and there's not a thing I could do to help them,' she said as she clung to the 3-year-old Susan. 'I thought once we moved from the dirt of the pit that you would all be safe, but it obviously hasn't got anything to do with where you live. I'll have to let your da know. Ann, will you pop along to Mr Thursby at the post office and ask him to send a message to your da telling him about our Mary Ann?'

'Aye, Ma, I'll go, and I'll take our Sarah and Susan with me, so you can have a bit of time on your own.'

'Thanks lass, I'll speak to Mr Thubron about a coffin.'

Mary Ann was buried alongside her brother and sister in St Cuthbert's churchyard. There was no marker to the grave and it was on the left of the main path leading to the church. The day of the funeral was really cold and only a few people turned up. The Revd Blenkinsopp said in his eulogy that he greatly regretted the number of children he was expected to bury in this district as their number was much higher than those of adult burials. Hannah listened with interest to this information. She was already asking why she had lost three children and Revd Blenkinsopp had confirmed that there was a problem with the number of children dying. Hannah's friend, Harriet Gray, or Jordan now that she was married, was a great support at this very sad time. Harriet's mother, Sarah, had been a friend of Hannah's mother from their Lumley days, and the family were now living near Hannah in Shadforth. Harriet offered to give details of Mary Ann's death to the registrar when he next visited Shadforth, and Hannah was only too pleased to pass on that responsibility.

Hannah was forced to get on with her life. She had her remaining children to look after, and with John away she was responsible for providing for them. He sent money every two weeks from Australia, which she collected from the post office, and together with her needlework tasks and Ralph's pay from the pit, the family were not badly off.

On 7 April 1861, John Sanderson from the farm knocked on Hannah's door. 'Hello Mrs Porter, I'm doing the census for Shadforth. I need to ask you some questions if that's all right?'

'Aye come in lad, I'll make us a cup of tea,' said Hannah. John settled himself at the table. He and Hannah chatted and drank their tea as they completed the form.

'I need to know who will be staying here tonight,' he said. 'Everybody in the country will be giving this information to somebody like me today.'

'Aye all right lad: there'll be me, our Ralph, Sarah and Susan.'

'Right, I also need their ages, including yours, and where you were all born.'

'Well I'm not afraid to tell you that I'm forty-one,' said Hannah, 'and I was born at Lumley. Our Ralph was born in Thornley, Sarah at Sherburn Hill and Susan − that's Susannah − at Paradise. Oh, and I've just remembered I'll have me nephew staying tonight. He's Thomas Porter and he's three from Sherburn Hill. Will you need to add him to the form?'

'Yes, everybody that stays in your house tonight. Right that's fine, I think I've got everything I need. I have to visit every house in Shadforth and Ludworth so I'd better be on my way. Thanks for the tea.'

'Eeh you're welcome lad. It was nice to see you and have a bit of a chat. Tell yer mother I'm asking after her.'

Hannah welcomed the summer this year as she and her children didn't have to work in the fields. They spent many happy hours out of doors, walking and picnicking in Shadforth Dene. Hannah was certain that fresh air must be the secret of good health and made sure that Ralph in particular spent as much time outside as possible when he wasn't at the pit.

On Saturday, 24 August 1861 Hannah and the girls walked over the fields to Thornley to attend a bazaar in aid of the Wesleyan Chapel fund. The event was held in the grounds of Thornley House, where the colliery manager lived. Once in the garden, a gate led into a field belonging to Farmer Ellison in which stood a 60ft-long tent that contained stalls and displays. By 11 a.m. the tent and the garden were packed with people taking advantage of the windy but warm weather and spending their money freely. The refreshment stall was particularly popular. They were selling beef, mutton, ham and tongues. At about 4 p.m. 450 people sat down to tea. Hannah and the girls had a great day meeting friends they hadn't seen for a while and catching up with everyone's news. After the tea was finished, loud cheering greeted the news that £60 4s 3d had been raised.

Shadforth village school.

During the rest of 1861 Ludworth pit laid the men off more times than enough. There were various rumours for the lay-offs; some said it was because the engine beam was dangerous, others that the pit was not economical. This state of affairs annoyed Ralph. He was a young man who wanted to work and he felt frustrated by the Ludworth owners, who were the same as those at Thornley pit who had so frustrated his father and grandfather twenty years earlier. 'I'm not staying there, Ma, they don't care about their workers.'

'You'll find that all owners are like that lad. Yer da did, that's one of the reasons he's in Australia.'

'Aye I know that, but I'm not prepared to move to Australia. I thought I might try Sherburn Hill. Me uncle Ralph thinks he can get me set on.'

'Well, give it a try, its six and two threes as far as travelling goes, and you can't be any worse off.'

'Aye, well I'm going over to try and get set on when the Bond starts again in March.'

Glass plate image of Hannah and her daughters, 1862.

Ralph got his job at Sherburn Hill pit in 1862 and daughter Susan started at the new Shadforth schoolroom in 1863. It was a church school supported by the Church of England and the master was Mr Barron. It was a small building of one room and a porch, while an attached cottage provided accommodation for the head-master. Hannah was determined that Susan would be educated; she always regretted her own lack of education and could see the merits of the three Rs that the school provided. Bible studies was also an important part of the curriculum. Susan was 6 years old when she started and the only one of Hannah's children to receive a formal education. Her sister, Sarah, attended Sunday school in Ludworth and loved hearing the stories told by the superintendent there, as well as learning to read and write. However, Hannah felt that Susan would be better off at the new school, and to celebrate the occasion Hannah took her and Sarah to have another photograph taken to send to John.

Hannah's father, Bill, died in 1864. He was working down the pit until 1861, when he was 74, but his health had been failing for some time and he and Ellen had moved to Ludworth at Hannah's suggestion while he was still working so that he would be eligible for a colliery house. Hannah was very surprised when her father took her advice and made the move to the neighbouring village. She had realised long ago that she took after her father in many respects and that both she and he would only do what they wanted to do. Bill had taken on surface work at Ludworth pit in line with his advancing years. Miners generally had to work until they died as there was no provision made for pensions or accommodation. If they became so ill that they couldn't work their families were expected to take the old people into their homes. Hannah and the family were able to keep an eye on Bill at Ludworth. Her brother, Ralph, and his family were at Sherburn Hill so there was never a shortage of people to visit Bill and Ellen. Bill died of bronchitis and was buried at Shadforth churchyard on 30 September. Hannah took the opportunity to say a little prayer at the grave of her children while in the churchyard.

Things plodded on until 1865, which was a big year for the Porters; it was the year that Ralph married. While working at Sherburn Hill he had met his sweetheart, Hannah Barron, and they married in St Lawrence's Church, Pittington, on 26 May. Once again, Hannah asked Mr Thursby at the post office to let husband John know about this happy occasion. She also arranged for Ralph to have his photograph taken to send to his father.

It was also the year that Ann and husband Billy had their third baby. Everyone concerned was worried by this third pregnancy – the second after the death of baby John in 1860 was a little girl born in 1863 and named Mary Ann, who only lived one year, but things were altogether different this time. Ann gave birth to the baby without too much trouble and they called him John Edward after both of their fathers, but he would be known as Jack.

The most momentous event that year, however, occurred just before Christmas. Hannah was working on her sewing in the living room of Seldom Seen when a knock came to the door. She put down her

Ralph Porter, born 1843.

work and opened the door to find a man there that she vaguely recognised. 'Well aren't you going to invite me in then?' he said.

'Eeh John, it can't be you?' She hardly recognised her husband sporting a full beard.

'It can and it is lass. I'm home at last.' Hannah reached forward and pulled John into the living room, tears of joy streaming down her face. 'Oh, it's so good to see you,' she said. 'I thought you were never coming home and there's so much happened while you've been away.'

'Aye I know, and one of them is you trying to hide from me in here. I left you in Paradise Row and come back to find you in somebody's back yard.'

'I thought I asked Mr Thursby to let you know I'd moved,' said Hannah.

'Well one of you forgot,' said John with a smile on his face. 'Neddy Baldwin told me just before I bowled into the cottage at Paradise.'

'Eeh I'm sorry John, that would have been so funny if you had. I couldn't do with working in the fields, it was back-breaking and our Ralph wanted to go to the pit and wouldn't be able to work for the Sandersons, so when I got the chance of this little place, I took it.'

'Well it's very cosy I must say,' said John. 'Now are you putting the kettle on?'

John had been on his way home for eight months and so all communications sent to him in Australia since April had missed him. As well as being unaware of the move of house, he didn't know about Ann's third baby and Ralph's marriage. 'Eeh such a lot's changed since I went away,' said John, 'but at least I was able to send regular money to see that you could live well. Where's the bairns? Are they due back?'

'Aye, our Susan's at school and will be back at four o'clock.'

'School, a proper school? Eeh that's grand, the first of our bairns to receive a proper education. Is she doing alright?'

'She loves it,' Hannah replied. 'She can read and write as good as anybody, and our Sarah's up at Sanderson's farm making some new curtains for Mary. She'll be back for her tea about four o'clock as well.'

'I've brought our Susan a big doll and a locket for our Sarah,' said John. Hannah had wondered what was in the long box John had brought with him and she wondered how it had survived life at sea for eight months. 'Oh, they'll be thrilled, although it'll be the first time our Susan's met you.'

At 4 p.m. both girls came running into the cottage together. 'Eeh, Ma, I could see our Sarah coming along through the village when I left the school, so I walked along to meet her,' said Susan, her cheeks glowing with the cold. Both girls stopped dead at the sight of the big bearded man sitting at their table. Eventually Sarah stepped towards him and said, 'Da, is that you, Da?' Before John had the chance to answer, Sarah threw herself into her father's arms. 'Eeh I recognised you,' said Sarah, 'after all this time, I still recognised you.'

'Aye you did lass, but it took you long enough,' laughed John, 'and you must be our little Susannah,' John said, holding his arms out for Susan, who was rather shy of this stranger. However, with Hannah's coaxing she eventually stepped forward to receive her first hug from her father. 'I've brought you both a present,' said John. He got up and picked up the big box and handed it to Susan. 'Eeh, Da, thank you,' said Susan, wide-eyed at the size of the box. She lifted the lid off to reveal the doll. 'I've never seen such a lovely doll, she looks just like a little girl. I can make some new clothes for her can't I, Ma?'

'Aye you can lass, she can have a range of rig-outs.'

'I didn't get you a doll Sarah lass because I knew you'd be a young lady by now, so I've bought you this. I'm told they're all the rage in Australia.' John produced a small box from his pocket and handed it to his elder daughter. Sarah opened it carefully to reveal the locket. 'Oh Da, it's beautiful! I've never had such a lovely present. I'll wear it all the time and I'll put an image of you and me ma in it.'

'Oh aye, I forgot about that,' said John. 'I was shocked to receive the images you sent me while I was away. I've managed to bring them back in one piece. It's a very clever invention and you must know somebody that could take more?'

'Oh aye, Mr Heaviside from Durham, he takes them. The next time I'm in Durham I'll ask him to take you and me ma for me locket.'

'Oh, you will, will you?' said Hannah. 'And who will be paying for that pleasure?'

'Well, I'll start saving and by the time I get into Durham, I should have enough,' replied Sarah.

'And if you haven't, I'll put the rest,' said John. 'After all I brought the locket.'

'Well nobody's asked me if I've bought a present for your ma,' smiled John after the girls had both had a good look at their gifts.

'Eeh da, have you?' asked Susan.

'Why of course I have. I wouldn't leave her out now, would I?'

'Well you shouldn't have bothered,' said Hannah. 'I don't need presents. It's enough that you've come back home in one piece, safe and sound.' John reached into his jacket pocket and took out a small round box that he presented to Hannah. 'Aw John, it's lovely,' said Hannah extracting a gold signet ring from the box. 'Ooh let us have a look,' said Susan and Sarah, looking at the little gold ring with 'Hannah Porter' engraved on it. 'Put it on ma,' urged Susan. Hannah put the ring on her forefinger, 'Well

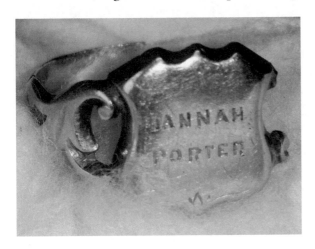

Hannah's signet ring.

99

I can always pawn it if we fall on hard times,' she joked. 'Aye you could an all, but you'd better not,' laughed John. Hannah was delighted with the ring, and like her wedding band, never took it off after that day.

Hannah sent a message to Ralph and Ann to tell them that John was home and by 6 o'clock the little cottage was packed with people and laughter. John was introduced to Ralph's wife, Hannah. 'Well it's lovely to meet you lass,' said John. 'I knew your da when we lived at Sherburn Hill, Bob isn't it?'

'Aye that's right Mr Porter, they still live there.'

'Well I'm pleased to hear it. Do you like living at Houghall, it seems a long way from here?'

'Aye, it's alright. We are staying with me ma in Sherburn tonight though, that's how we were able to get here. They were taking on at Houghall just after we got married and Ralph thought he might get a better cavil there.'

'Aye well he'll not be the first pitman to be looking for a better cavil. Believe it or not, it was the same in Australia. I was on the move regularly while I was there, looking for a better opportunity but I think it'll be the same as here – there isn't one for the working man. Exploitation is the best you can expect in our line of work.'

'Well he'll have to settle himself down until the bairn's born early next year, I don't want to be on the move with a little un.'

The cavilling system operated within the coal mines in order to try and make a difficult situation fair. The coal was easy to find in some districts of a pit and therefore a miner working there would have no trouble making money, whereas in other districts the conditions might be poor and working there would restrict earnings. In order to make the system fair, quarterly lots, known as cavils, were drawn to give the men the opportunity of a 'good' workplace and a 'poor' workplace.

John was thrilled with Ann's baby, Jack, and while Ann was not his natural daughter, he thought of her as family, as she did of him. 'I called him after you you know, Da?'

'Aye, I thought you did lass,' said John, 'and I'm honoured. He's a bonny little fella, with a good pair of lungs on him.' They both laughed as the baby opened his mouth to let out a cry.

'I'll go and see what he wants, he probably wants feeding. I cannot fill him at the moment,' said a proud Ann.

That night when their guests had left and the family had settled down for the night, John and Hannah were in the four-poster bed, 'It's good to be home and to be sleeping in such style. You'll never know how good it was to see all our growing family. I missed our Mary Ann though, she should have been with us. There were times when I was away when I thought I'd never see home again.'

'Did you not think Australia would be right for us then?' asked Hannah.

'No, I didn't. Like I was saying earlier, it was just the same as here only warmer. In fact, it was too hot at times. Workers are still exploited by the mine owners over there and as our family here was growing, I couldn't see you wanting to leave England.'

'Oh lad, let's be thankful. You're home safe and sound and you can see we're all happy to have you here. You're right though, I couldn't uproot to Australia, but I'm pleased we're both of one mind and we've had a good night welcoming you back.'

'Aye we have,' said John. 'There's just one thing that we'll have to put right.'

'Oh, and what's that?' said Hannah

'We'll have to get out of this shoebox of a cottage. There isn't room for a man to turn round.' They both laughed at this statement, but Hannah knew he was right. Seldom Seen had been fine for her and the children, but John looked out of place in the small rooms – he looked like a giant.

Christmas 1865 was a very happy time for the Porter family, but things changed the following year, and not for the better.

10

BACK TO THE BEGINNING

Early in 1866 John Porter was set on at Ludworth pit, which had recently passed into the ownership of London coal merchants Ralph Walton and John Gowland (the London Steam Collier and Coal Company Ltd). The land was leased to the new company by land owners Messrs Spearman, Wilkinson, Standish & Gowland and covered an area of between 3,000 and 4,000 acres; the landowners owning royalty rights to the coal beneath that would make them rich men. Walton and Gowland were originally from County Durham but carried on their coal exporting business in London, using their good connections with the County Durham owners to attract trade. It was planned to ship the coal from Ludworth via the port of Sunderland on a fleet of steamers ordered to be built at the Clyde shipyards. The Ludworth community felt confident that this would be the start of better times for their industry.

The colliery house allocated to the Porters was in 3rd Cross Row and was identical to the one they had occupied in Thornley. Hannah and John knew most of the people in the small village of Ludworth, and they all came out to watch the four-poster bed being delivered to the pit cottage. Hannah had become so attached to the bed that she asked Mr Thubron if she could buy it from him. However, it seems Mr Thubron was so pleased to get rid of it that he gave it to the Porters.

Ludworth pit.

The bed had to be dismantled by Mr Thubron to get it out of the cottage in Shadforth and he rebuilt it in the parlour of the colliery cottage in Ludworth. It is fair to say that the bed took up the whole of the room. Hannah had made new red velvet drapes for it and renewed the red carpet that covered the steps. 'This bed is far too big for this room,' said John, squeezing his way into the bedroom.

'Aye it is, but it's staying,' said Hannah. 'I've come to love this bed, and I'm not getting rid of it. It's got our feather mattress on it that we've had since we got married.' John, like most miners, wasn't at all interested in household matters, so he let the subject drop and had to admit that getting to sleep through the day was a bit easier in the big bed when the drapes were closed to provide extra darkness.

The family soon settled back into life in the colliery village, where dirt and grime were a way of life, and there was something that hadn't been part of their life in Shadforth. Domestic water in Ludworth was provided by a tap at the pit coal depot after it had been pumped from the pit. For some inhabitants of the village, this meant a walk of 350 yards to collect water. Hannah and her family were used to this inconvenience and were not shocked either at the way in which waste was disposed of in cesspits around the village, causing a horrendous smell in the summer weather.

In February disaster struck the family again. Their daughter Sarah, aged 14, died of the disease that had killed her siblings, phthisis, and she was buried alongside them in the grave at Shadforth churchyard. Hannah and John were once again devastated by the loss of a child, or a young woman as Sarah had become. She was a Sunday scholar at the chapel in Ludworth, two converted pit cottages run by superintendent George Cooke. The

VERSES ON THE DEATH OF
SARAH PORTER,

Who was a Sunday Scholar in Ludworth School,

BUT DIED FEBRUARY THE 17TH 1866,
AGED FOURTEEN YEARS.

1 Friends, while we stand before you here,
   This Anniversary Day,
With solemn reverence now give ear,
   To what I'm going to say.

2 Now Sarah Porter long has been,
   A Sabbath Scholar here,
Her age was only fourteen,
   Dear friends we loved her dear.

3 Just fourteen times all deck'd in green,
   Poor Sarah liv'd to see,
Just fourteen summers she had seen,
   And quickly did they flee.

4 When Stark and Walker with her prayed,
   Her heart in love did melt,
She talk'd to them and mildly said,
   She happy, happy felt.

5 To some she said, I'm going home,
   That home by far the best,
Where pain and death can never come,
   I go and there shall rest.

6 She's left a father and a mother,
   Here in this world of woe,
Two sisters dear, and a brother,
   To mourn her loss below.

7 Is Sarah gone? O yes she's dead!
   Her sufferings all are past,
Her spirit now is beautified,
   That beauty ever lasts.

8 Though buried deep in earth's dark womb,
   Her fading body lies,
Jesus will call her from the tomb,
   Yes friends she shall arise.

9 Her grave is now a downy bed,
   T'was dotted round with blood,
Then say no more that Sarah's dead,
   She only rests in God.

10 O think friends while we worship here,
   Her little harps she's stringing,
With love tones in her voice so clear,
   Her Saviour's love is singing.

11 With palms that's always glittering bright,
   Her crown fades not away,
She lives a seraph high in light,
   In heaven's long sunny day.

12 Her body sweetly rests in hope,
   Though greedy worms destroy;
Jesus at last will bring her up,
   And will increase her joy.

13 Though Sarah from us now has gone,
   She's free from every care,
She lives in heaven along with him,
   Who died to bring her there.

14 Then mourn no more tho' she is not,
   If you each be the Lord's,
He'll bless you with her happy lot,
   Which only heaven affords.

15 Rejoice her sufferings all are o'er,
   Disease with all its pain,
All past and she will die no more,
   Our loss is now her gain.

16 High in the heavenly world above,
   She swells yon happy crowd,
To sing for ever, God is love,
   In heavenly anthems loud.

17 Dear friends we cannot tell to day,
   What to morrow's dawning brings,
O Jesus draw our hearts away,
   Away from earthly things.

18 Time will not wait for us, stay
   It carries us along,
O waft us to the sun's bright day,
   The heavenly hosts among.

19 To day, dear Lord, to thee we come,
   Thou heard what each did say,
O Lord send none despairing home,
   Send none unblest away.

20 And may this memorable day,
   Long, long, remember'd be,
You've heard, and may we ever pray
   In death, remember me.

By GEORGE COOKE.

From G. Procter's City Steam Printing Offices, Market Place, Durham.

Verses on the life of Sarah Porter.

amount of child mortality was very depressing during the nineteenth century, particularly among the working classes and it is difficult to understand what the emotional impact of loss had on a family and on a community. We tend to think of grief as being private, but the discovery of a document has forced me to rethink that theory.

Procter's steam-printing offices, Market Place, Durham.

A handbill headed 'Verses on the Death of Sarah Porter, who was a Sunday Scholar in Ludworth School, but died 17 February 1866 aged 14 years' was produced by Mr Cooke of Ludworth. He wrote twenty religious verses all about the life (and death) of Sarah. Each verse gives us a little insight into her life; it mentions her friends, her family and the illness that killed her. The written notes were taken to Durham by Mr Cooke to be printed at G. Procter's steam-printing offices in Durham Market Place and distributed throughout the village of Ludworth as a handbill. These actions give a feeling of community grief over the death of this girl, which has clearly shocked them. In the verses, her life is publicly valued, and her individual memory celebrated. It is a rare document and one that Hannah and John would not be able to read but would enjoy having read to them. It was obviously a treasured document as the original still exists today.

The death of another of their daughters affected John and Hannah badly. After all, Sarah was 14, and her image on the glass slide image taken in 1862 shows her as a pretty, healthy-looking girl. Having lost three previous children at a much younger age, they may have felt that they would be more prepared to deal with her death, but this was not the case. Neither felt able to register the death of their daughter with the superintendent registrar, and this was left to son Ralph's mother-in-law, Alice Barron, who lived near the grieving family. Mrs Barron stated on Sarah's death certificate that she was present at the death, and no doubt the family were grateful for her help at that time and afterwards.

It is hard to gauge the emotional impact on Hannah. There is no evidence to suggest how Hannah felt. The whole community appeared to be grieving for Sarah Porter. Hannah sat day after day, clutching a bookmark that Sarah had embroidered to go into her Bible. It had the inscription 'Sweet Home – There's No Place Like Home' and her name, Sarah Porter. The words on the bookmark appear to be an indication of how happy Sarah was with her home life. There is no date to tell us when it was embroidered, but it signifies her happiness.

The grieving process was still going on at the end of March when Ralph's wife, Hannah, gave birth to their first son, who they named John after his paternal grandfather, and the sight of the new baby eventually drew Hannah out of her grief. Bit by bit, she regained her strength and managed to carry on as before as the hardworking, caring, leader of their family. Women were mostly the dominant adult in pit

Bookmark embroidered by Sarah Porter.

families. The man may have mended shoes and reported house repairs to the colliery office but, apart from requesting coal deliveries, this was the extent of his contribution to family life. Men often had an allotment, and some went to the pub or chapel, but it was the women who became the main parent and household manager.

On Saturday, 28 April, the miners and their families from Thornley and Ludworth were invited by the new owners of the pit to a day of feasting and rejoicing as had never been seen before in the two villages. John, Hannah and Susan were there, as were Ralph and his family and Ann and Billy Baldwin. Banners were flying in the pit yard at Thornley where the event was held, and cannon were fired at short intervals. The South Hetton brass band marched through Thornley and helped create a holiday spirit. All work at the pit was suspended for the day so that everyone could enjoy the festivities. At 12 noon about 900 workmen sat down to dinner in the pit yard on tables specially laid out for the occasion. The fitting shops were adorned with flags and festoons of evergreens and the band played on a specially set up platform. Tea was provided for the women and children. They were not included in the dinner arrangements, an indication of the lack of importance shown to them by the great men who were about to save the coal industry in Thornley and Ludworth.

The new owners made several speeches to reassure the men that their situation would improve – they promised on that day to try and make the miners' homes more comfortable and to lead water into the streets. The new directors had been told that Thornley and Ludworth were the worst colliery villages on the face of the earth and their people were drunken, low and squalid. However, they changed their minds after meeting with the mining families. In one of the speeches, they informed those present about two steamers they had ordered from the shipyards on the Clyde and told them that the two boats would be named *The Ludworth* and *The Thornley*.

Unfortunately, in June of the same year, news reached the two villages that the shipyard making the two steamers, along with others along the Clyde, had closed as a result of strike action. This would seriously set back the plans for the Thornley and Ludworth coal. However, the new owners remained popular with the miners and Mr J. Smith, a hewer at both collieries, wrote to the *Durham Chronicle* to point out that Mr Gowland & Co. were as good as their word in respect of trying to improve the miners' lives. They had arranged for a locomotive engine to transport the men to and from the pit. This action was well received by the miners and Mr Smith, acting as their spokesperson, offered his hearty thanks to the company.

Susan Porter was sorry to hear that the headmaster of the Ludworth School that she attended would be leaving at the end of 1868. She had settled in well from the school in Shadforth, and thought Mr Leitch was very kind to the children. He told an assembly in school that he was moving to St Andrew's School at Hebburn Quay.

Ludworth and Thornley pits went on strike again in 1869 and as far as John Porter was concerned, it was history repeating itself. 'This is the very reason I moved from this coal company in the first place, because of the way in which they treat their workers, and even though there's been a change of ownership, it's still the same. I can't believe we're still striking over the Bond.'

'Do you wish you'd sent for us in Australia then?' asked Hannah.

'No, it wasn't much better there with regard to work, but it was always warm – too warm at times and, like I've said before, I was changing my job regularly looking for a good employer, but it was the same as here. I had a good look around but on balance I felt we were better off here. As I've already told you, I spent some time working in a gold mine, but their owners were just the same. Then once the bairns started to get married, I knew you wouldn't want to leave.'

In 1873 Hannah and John were presented with their first grand-daughter, the first daughter of their son Ralph and his wife. They called her Sarah, no doubt after Ralph's sister. Hannah and John were proud and delighted with the new arrival.

Over the next few months, John must have regretted his decision to return to work at Ludworth pit many times, as the company responsible for Ludworth, Wheatley Hill and Thornley pits lurched from one crisis to another and at one point Ludworth pit was put up for sale. There were strikes, lockouts and meetings. John was so tired of it all, he didn't get involved in the ins and outs of why. He went to the pit, on the days it was working, with a heavy heart, wishing he had some other way of making money for his family. There was only Susan living at home now – she was 17 in 1874, a dressmaker like her mother and a very pretty girl.

There was to be a grand gala at Thornley on Monday, 10 August 1874 and it appeared that everyone in Ludworth would be going to it. It was to be a day of sports, music, sideshows and refreshments. Hannah and Susan had been looking forward to this event for weeks. John was non-committal, but Hannah insisted that he went with them. The event was held in Mr Ellison's field behind Gore Hall Farm and the weather in the morning was changeable; however, by lunch-time the sun had come out and the sky didn't have a cloud it in. As a result of the good weather, by 1 p.m. the event was full of mining families intent on having a good time.

Music was provided by the twenty-six-strong band of the *Wellesley* training ship from North Shields. They were loudly applauded after every piece of music. The sports started at 2 p.m. and the most popular event was the cuddy race. Sgt Scott and his band of police officers were on hand to put a stop to any illegal gambling. There was a quoits competition, a race for draught horses and a donkey race, which caused great amusement among the crowd. The Porters watched the foot racing, pole leaping and the three-legged race, and enjoyed the refreshments provided.

It was a perfect day. Ann and Billy, now living at Trimdon, came over to join their family for the day and Ralph and Hannah from Houghall.

It was a lovely family occasion that went on until 8 p.m., when the revellers said their goodbyes and headed for home. 'Eeh I'm pleased you nagged me to come along today,' said John, 'I've really enjoyed it.'

'Well you don't know what's good for you,' laughed Hannah.

'It's been a lovely day, Ma. I enjoyed everything, especially being with my friends.'

'Oh aye, and any friend in particular?' asked her father.

'No, Da, just my friends.'

'Well I thought young Jakey Jopling was showing quite an interest in your friendship.'

'Jakey? No, Da, I've known him for ages, we're all friends together.' John and Hannah exchanged a knowing look and let the matter drop.

11

TROUBLE IN TWOS

When John came home from the pit on Tuesday, he told Hannah that the new union was advising the workers to join the Permanent Relief Fund. 'What's that then?' asked Hannah.

'Well as far as I can make out, you pay fortnightly into the scheme and if I have an accident at the pit and die, you will get a lump sum called compensation, and a pension.'

'But what if you don't have an accident at the pit?'

'Well you won't need a lump sum or a pension, will you?'

'But what happens to the money we've paid in?'

'Nothing, it just stays in the scheme and others will benefit from it.'

'Seems like a risk to me,' said Hannah, 'paying for something that you might never use.'

'On the other hand, if we do need it, it's the only payment you'll get. The owners won't pay out compensation or pensions, you know that.'

'Aye, I know that, but I hope we don't ever need anything like that.'

'And so do I lass, but you know as well as I do the amount of accidents that happens down the pit, you can never tell.'

The Permanent Relief Fund was set up to provide miners with financial help in the event of an accident or death, at a time when the private owners could always find a way of suggesting that the death or injury was 'accidental' and therefore not liable for a compensation payment. Trade unionism was quite new in the Durham coalfield and their local representatives were spreading the message of this fund, telling the men, 'Make this investment in yourselves, it might be the only thing available to you and your families if you have an accident at the pit.' Attitudes like those of Hannah were common, however, but the miners themselves were keen to get involved to provide for their families in the event of an accident. After more discussion, John convinced Hannah that it was the right thing to do and he arranged to join the scheme.

John went to work as usual on Friday, 6 November 1874 and was preparing to leave the pit at about 3 p.m. He was at the pit bottom waiting for the cage – a three-decker. When the cage arrived, the tubs were pulled out and John attempted to get into the space that they left. The cage moved while he was getting in and a marra, John Jones, tried to pull him out of the cage and get him back but his right leg got fastened between the cage and the scaffold. John was carried home and Dr Nesbitt sent for, but he died from the injury five days after the accident.

When they brought John home from the pit on a stretcher on the Friday, Hannah had no idea how serious his injury was. Dr Nesbitt called later and told her he would have liked to have amputated John's right leg, which would have saved his life, but was worried about him being in shock. The doctor explained to Hannah that shock is a life-threatening medical condition as a result of insufficient blood flow throughout the body and was common after a severe injury. The doctor explained that medical shock can lead to other conditions such as lack of oxygen in the body's tissues and lead to heart attack or organ damage. There was very little Dr Nesbitt could do about the shock – he advised Hannah to keep John warm and calm and get him to drink plenty of fluids. Of course, Hannah included her comfrey remedy to the fluids given to John over those few days he was lying in agony. He slipped into a deep sleep on the afternoon before he died and didn't regain consciousness. He died in the four-poster bed in the parlour of their colliery house surrounded by his family.

Ann, Ralph and Susan, John's only surviving children, were present, as well as Hannah. Ann and Susan made numerous cups of tea for those

Headstone of John Porter and family.

coming round to mourn John's death, and Lizzie Hartley was sent for to lay him out.

The funeral was planned for Friday, 13 November at St Cuthbert's Church in Shadforth in the same grave as his four children. The family walked from Ludworth to Shadforth, and John's coffin was taken by a cart from Shadforth Hill House Farm, courtesy of the Sandersons. Mrs Sanderson had died a few years back, in 1872, but the lads never forgot their ties with the Porter family. With her money from the Permanent Relief Fund, Hannah bought a headstone for the grave and had the names of everyone it held engraved on it. 'Eeh, Ma, are you sure you want to spend your money on a headstone?' daughter Ann asked.

'Aye I am lass, I wouldn't have had the money if it hadn't been for your da. He must have known that something like this was going to happen, so I'm going to have a stone with it.'

The Ludworth Inn.

An inquest was held at the Ludworth Inn on Saturday, 14 November. Crofton Maynard, the coroner, was present along with James Willis, Inspector of Mines. Dr Nesbitt said he knew the deceased, who was 64 years old. Throughout the proceedings John was referred to as 'an old man'. The doctor said he visited John on Sunday, 8 November and found that he had a large lacerated wound on his right leg that extended about four inches from his knee to three inches below. He also had a bruise over his right hip. Dr Nesbitt attended John until his death on 11 November. He told the inquest that he couldn't amputate the leg as John didn't recover from the shock of the accident.

There was some suggestion that the onsetter may have committed a gross breach of the special rules of the colliery by signalling to bank and that John lost his life through it. As a result, the coroner suggested that this may have attracted a charge of manslaughter, but John had attempted to enter the cage improperly, therefore contributing to his own death. A verdict of accidental death was returned by the jury. John would not have been surprised by this verdict – in fact, he would have expected it.

Christmas 1874 was a very sombre affair for the Porters. Hannah had moved out of her colliery house within the two-week period allowed after John's death. She and daughter Susan moved to Shadforth Terrace in Ludworth, a private rented house. Both concentrated on their dressmaking full-time now as they were the only breadwinners. Hannah was 54, Susan 17. As her father had predicted, Susan's friendship with Jake Jopling was developing and having lost his mother a few years before, when he was 16, Jake was a great comfort to Susan after the loss of her father. Hannah did not like the developing relationship. She didn't encourage any discussion about Jake and her reasons were simple, to her. His grandparents, Jack and Annie Jamieson, ran the top house, the local name for the Ludworth Inn, and Hannah was against anybody so closely linked to alcohol.

Susan thought this was very unfair. 'But he doesn't even live there!'

'I know he doesn't, he lives with his da behind the shop in North View, but he's bound to be close to Jack and Annie, his grandparents. They were his mother's parents.'

'Yes, but he doesn't even drink in the top house,' argued Susan.

'Not yet,' replied Hannah, indicating that the conversation was over.

'Well I'm not going to stop seeing him, Ma, I don't care what you say. I like Jake and he likes me and just because you don't like alcohol isn't a good enough reason.'

Hannah didn't reply. She knew Jake's family and she had known his mother, Rachel, a nice woman who came from a large Ludworth family. Hannah had been lucky; John liked a drink but he wasn't a drinker. She had never seen him the worse for wear as a result of drink, but she had seen how it had ruined lives. She'd seen the effect on her neighbours whose men did drink and came home on pay Friday without their pay because they'd drunk it in the pub, or they'd gambled it away whilst drunk. Even worse, she had witnessed men coming home drunk on pay Friday having spent his money and beating their wives and bairns, driven by their own guilt. It had been a feature of her life – she had seen this wherever she had lived. There was a fortnight stretching out in front of these families before the next pay day, with no money to pay for food.

Hannah's mother and then she herself had always helped a woman in these circumstances, and did so gladly, but Hannah was determined her youngest daughter was not going to walk into a situation where drink could ruin the rest of her life. This was to cause problems between Hannah and Susan over the next few years as Susan's friendship with Jake developed and looked as if it would lead to marriage.

At the end of the year, Ludworth was buzzing with gossip. 'Apparently, one of Bill Jopling's lads has robbed his grandmother of £90,' Hannah told Susan.

'Do you know which lad it was?' asked Susan.

'Aye, it was young Lance; he's the good runner isn't he?' Lance was five years older than Jake.

'Yes, Lance is a good runner, he's won prizes, but I bet you're disappointed it was him?' said Susan. 'You could have had a field day if it had been Jake, robbing from his family.'

'Aye, well as I've said before, you want nothing to do with them.'

'Well, Lance was staying at the pub with his granny as it was just after the death of his granda,' said Susan, 'so it might be a misunderstanding.'

'He's been to court at Castle Eden, that's how much of a misunderstanding it is,' said Hannah. Susan knew she wouldn't be able to win over her mother. She asked Jake about the gossip the next time she saw him. He was clearly embarrassed and said, 'Aye, after our Lance went to court, me granny says she found the money so there was no further action.'

'Oh, that's good,' said Susan, willing to believe the best in his family to keep her mother off her back. She did realise though in the weeks that followed that Jake's relationship with Lance cooled and Jake rarely mentioned his name.

During early 1875 Hannah became involved in raising money for a new chapel in Ludworth. The Primitive Methodists held services and a Sunday school in the village and had done for some years in two miners' cottages set aside for religion. Hannah's daughter, Sarah, had been a Sunday scholar there, but the time had come to try to build a chapel with the increase in the population.

On 1 and 2 May 1875 Ludworth hosted an event intended to raise money for the building of the chapel. About 500 people sat down to a tea held in a tent pitched in a field owned by Mr Ramsay of Tower Farm. There were stalls selling food, clothing and fancy goods. The

Haswell choir sang throughout and were greatly admired by visitors. On the Sunday three sermons were preached in the morning and evening and attracted many visitors. £50 was raised over the two days. Hannah and Susan, along with other women from the village, helped provide the tea and spent a busy few days, baking and then helping out at the event itself. It seemed the whole village was there as a result of good weather, and for all there was some snowfall during May, the first weekend was fine and sunny.

Hannah caught sight of Susan sitting with Jakey during the Saturday afternoon, but they weren't on their own, they were with other young people from Ludworth and Hannah felt it would be wiser not to interfere and spoil the day for everybody. On the whole, she and Susan were getting on just fine without John. They were spending time dressmaking in order to pay the rent and they had a lodger, whose money helped out, too. The only blight on the relationship was Susan's determination to see the Jopling lad.

In June 1875 the innkeeper of the Queen's Head at Ludworth was killed at the pit in a similar way to John. He was jammed by the cage down the pit. Hearing of this accident brought it all back to Hannah and the conversations she and John had had over the years about the negligence of the coal owners and their attitude to health and safety. She now feared for her son, Ralph, who after the death of his father had moved his family from Houghall to Ludworth to be near his mother. Hannah hoped Ralph would be safe in the pit.

In July, Ralph, along with others, were charged under the Masters and Servants Act with neglecting to fulfil their contract with the coal company. It appears that the men came out on strike as they had been paid short, despite an agreement with the owners being in place. The case was heard at Castle Eden Magistrates' Court on Saturday, 17 July and adjourned to a later date while discussions were carried out with the union and the men. The charges were eventually dropped at the beginning of August, an amicable settlement of the dispute being arrived at. Hannah was relieved. She was annoyed at Ralph for getting involved in striking but he was like his father, and hated the unfairness dealt out to the pitmen by the owners.

Hannah was busy with affairs of the chapel again in August when a two-day music festival was held to raise money for the building. The Easington Lane choral society and the Wheatley Hill and Haswell Primitive Methodist choirs performed several selections of music that were enjoyed by about 500 people. Tea was served after the music and then a public meeting was held. Once again Hannah was exhausted after such a busy weekend. The only downside to the event was the heavy rain that started at about 4 p.m. on the second day and drenched everyone and everything. People waited inside the tent until the rain stopped before making their way back to the village.

Upon reaching home, Hannah could see that something was wrong; she could see front doors standing open and those people in two-storey accommodation like hers were leaning out the bedroom windows. It appeared that the whole of Ludworth was flooded. Her own house was under 2ft of water. 'Oh my dear God, my four-poster bed; I do hope the water won't get upstairs,' Hannah thought as she hurried towards the house.

Susan greeted her at the door, 'Eh, Ma, if it hadn't been for me and Jakey, our furniture would have floated away. We've carried most of it upstairs.' Hannah forgot that she didn't approve of Jakey and at this moment he had been her saviour.

'Thanks lad, I don't know what I would have done without you,' said Hannah, and she meant it.

'It's alright Mrs Porter, you're pretty low down here, that's why you've had it worse than the rest of the village. You'll be alright upstairs until the rain stops and the water goes back, if you and Susan can keep the fire going. The furniture wouldn't have floated away, it wasn't that deep,' Jake replied, smiling at Hannah.

'Aye we can manage to keep the fire going lad, and I know our Susan's one for exaggerating, now off you go, your da will be wondering where you are.'

'Can he not stay a bit longer, Ma?' asked Susan hopefully.

'No, it wouldn't be right Susan, not tonight, not when we have to stay upstairs.'

'It's alright Mrs Porter. I'll see you tomorrow Susan,' and Jakey left the deep waters of Shadforth Terrace to make his way to North View.

The whole place was under water. The road to Sherburn Hill and Haswell Plough were both closed as a result of flooding and the only way out of the village of Ludworth was to Thornley, along the line. Those in single-storey cottages had had to move into the homes of family and friends who had an upstairs or a dry house. It took a few days for the water to subside, but eventually the villagers got back to normal.

It was a great day for the village when Ludworth Primitive Methodist Chapel opened on Saturday, 11 November 1876. Once again it was a day of celebrating, and Hannah and the other women of the village provided tea and refreshments for the great numbers of people who came to hear the three sermons preached throughout the day.

On 18 January 1877 disaster struck the Thornley, Ludworth and Wheatley Hill area when their coal company, the Original Hartlepool Collieries Company, went into liquidation. The company didn't have enough money to meet the wages bill and the area fell into a deep depression. The miners were allowed to stay in their homes for the time being, but once a buyer was found, if one was, but no one knew what the future held. Hannah and Susan were hit by the loss of their lodger's money, as he moved out as soon as the pit closed and went to seek work elsewhere. Even worse for Susan, Jakey's father arranged for him to get set on at Brandon pit and live there with his aunt, Elizabeth Stephenson, his mother's sister. He would be living at 2 West Terrace, Peases, West Brandon. Susan was devastated, although Hannah thought it was the best thing that could have happened. He might meet a lass over there and marry her, after all he was 23 now.

Many Ludworth residents drifted away to find work at other pits, and the ones that stayed were starving by March 1877. They were disillusioned by the new union, which ruled that the men would receive 8s per week but only for eight weeks. Donations were requested from other areas of the coalfield and a total of £119 15s was raised. To make matters worse, the pit deputies left the Durham Miners Association to join their own, newly formed, union, which was paying 12s per week per man and 2s per head for children. This caused trouble in the village − it set man against man and family against family.

𝔓𝔞𝔯𝔱𝔦𝔠𝔲𝔩𝔞𝔯𝔰, 𝔓𝔩𝔞𝔫 𝔞𝔫𝔡 ℭ𝔬𝔫𝔡𝔦𝔱𝔦𝔬𝔫𝔰 𝔬𝔣 𝔖𝔞𝔩𝔢

Of that Important and well known current going sea sale Colliery,

CALLED THE

LUDWORTH COLLIERY,

In the County of DURHAM,

(The property of the "Original Hartlepool Collieries Company," Limited),

CONTAINING

527a. 2r. 9p. or thereabouts,

(LYING TO THE NORTH OF THE WHIN DYKE)

TOGETHER WITH THE

COLLIERY PLANT,

OF

Pits, Engine Houses, Engines, Machinery, Railways, Screens,
Stores, Materials,

LIVE AND DEAD STOCK,

Agents and Workmen's Houses, Workshops, Stables, Granaries, and all other
Erections and Buildings whatsoever, to the same Colliery belonging or
appertaining, and held therewith,

𝔄𝔩𝔩 𝔬𝔣 𝔴𝔥𝔦𝔠𝔥 𝔴𝔦𝔩𝔩 𝔟𝔢 𝔬𝔣𝔣𝔢𝔯𝔢𝔡 𝔣𝔬𝔯 𝔖𝔞𝔩𝔢 𝔟𝔶 𝔄𝔲𝔠𝔱𝔦𝔬𝔫,

IN ONE LOT,

BY

Mr. CHAS. BROUGH,

AT THE "QUEEN'S HEAD HOTEL,"

PILGRIM STREET, NEWCASTLE-UPON-TYNE,

On TUESDAY, the 12th day of DECEMBER, 1871,

AT TWO O'CLOCK IN THE AFTERNOON PRECISELY.

Particulars with Plan and Conditions of Sale, may be had (gratis), and further information obtained
on application to Mr. PHILIP COOPER, Viewer, Thornley Colliery; Messrs. HARCOURT AND
MACARTHUR, 8, Moorgate Street, London, Solicitors; of T. R. EAMES, Esq., St. Michael's House,
St. Michael's Alley, Cornhill, London, and of the Auctioneer.
The Colliery may be viewed on application to Mr. COOPER.

Sale notice for Ludworth pit.

Meetings were held and letters written to the *Durham Chronicle* high-lighting the plight of the miners at Thornley, Ludworth and Wheatley Hill who were still owed wages from January. An auction of the pits was held at the Turk's Head Hotel, Newcastle, on 9 August 1877, but despite a large attendance of colliery owners and gentlemen of the district no bids were forthcoming.

12

HERE COME THE BRIDES

Susan was twenty-one in 1878 – she was coming of age. Parents were the main moral guides for working-class girls and on achieving this birthday Susan might expect some lessening of the guide ropes, and may even expect to make some decisions about her own future. However, this was not to be. Hannah was still dead set against Jake Jopling and never missed an opportunity to say so. Her continued bad feeling towards Jake, rather than turn Susan against him, made her all the more determined to see him, even though he was still living on the other side of Durham.

Hannah invited close family for a tea party on Susan's birthday and she presented her daughter with twenty-four solid silver spoons – twelve teaspoons and twelve dessert spoons, each piece engraved with Susan's initials. Hannah was acknowledging that marriage was the next logical step in her daughter's life and the gift was to start off her 'bottom drawer'. This is another occasion when Hannah's behaviour was probably unexpected. She was a widow in receipt of a small pension, making money from dressmaking and yet able to buy a cutlery set that must have cost about £10. There will have been the opportunity for Hannah to buy this item on credit from the travellers who visited the colliery villages from Sunderland stores. Most of the miners bought large or luxury items by this method, putting down a deposit and then making a fortnightly payment when the agent came to collect each pay Friday.

This is how many of the men obtained their pocket watches and the occasional piece of mahogany furniture. Susan was delighted with the gift but unsure if Jake would ever see it.

Hannah continued her work with the Primitive Methodist Chapel and helped provide the tea for a special event there in September 1878 when 300 people sat down for a meal that was reported in the *Durham Chronicle* as 'in a first-rate style'. The women of the committee had become firm friends and met regularly to discuss catering arrangements. Hannah was glad of the distraction from her sewing and looked forward to the events, where she felt she was making a difference by providing something to look forward to for the community.

In the absence of a buyer the pit continued to work but not on full strength and the accidents continued, hence Hannah was pleased when she heard that Mr Cooper, the agent of Thornley, Ludworth and Wheatley Hill collieries, had appeared at the Castle Eden Petty Sessions just before Christmas 1878, charged with having an exposed and dangerous part of machinery insecurely fenced. He was fined £5 and the three villages were buzzing with the news. This was the first time that the owners (or their representatives) had been brought to account for their dangerous practices.

'Oh I wish John had been here to see this day,' Hannah told her friend, Lizzie Archer, as they walked through Ludworth on their way to the chapel. 'He hated the owners for the dangerous way they ran the pits, and it cost him his life.'

'I know, my man is a deputy and he's always complaining. He says it's a wonder not more men are killed in the pits. He was saying last night that Bill Jopling's son is taking the owners to court.'

This was music to Hannah's ears. 'Which son would that be? He has four I believe.'

'Oh the one that's the checkweighman, and very highly thought of in the pit. He believes the owners have acted illegally in keeping the men's wages from them since January.'

Hannah knew that Will Jopling, Jake's brother, was held in high esteem by the men of Ludworth pit. They got to choose their own checkweighman because he was the man who weighed the tubs of coal when they came to bank and allocated the correct payment to the correct miners. It was a job requiring trust and honesty. The men were paid on the say-so of the checkweighman.

Hannah lost interest when she knew it was Will. He was, she knew, very popular within Ludworth because of his honesty and integrity. The men at the pit admired him for standing up to the owners. He was a very clever man and would probably run rings around the coal owner's representatives in court.

Life went on as normal for the residents of Ludworth during the rest of the 1870s. Hannah continued her involvement with the chapel and she and Susan with their needlework. The friendship between Susan and Jakey continued without Hannah's blessing, and when she heard in June that Jake had appeared before the magistrate charged with trespassing, Hannah was delighted. 'He was only fined a shilling, Ma, and he really did think the road through Mr Hunter's farm was a right of way.'

'Well obviously it wasn't,' replied Hannah, 'and it just shows what sort of lad he is – out to get his own way.'

'It doesn't matter what he does, you're never going to like him are you?'

'You're probably right lass, and I'd be a lot happier if you didn't like him either.'

At the end of 1880 Hannah got a shock when Lizzie Archer died suddenly. She was only 47. Despite the age difference, Lizzie and Hannah had become friends through their work at the chapel. Lizzie already had eight bairns and her death was due to another pregnancy, which, at 47, was too much for her. She died before the birth, losing the baby at the same time. The three oldest children were married and so Lizzie's husband, John, was left with five at home.

There was better news for the area in July 1881 when the Thornley and Wheatley Hill collieries were taken over by a Mr Ford from London. He at once settled the money owing to the men from 1878 in return for them starting work. He made it plain, however, that the pit would not be running at full capacity for a few more weeks until he had made an assessment of the workings. Mr Ford was anxious to take possession of Ludworth colliery and settle with the men in the same way he had settled with those of Wheatley Hill, and the Ludworth pit eventually recommenced work in August 1881.

Hannah had more to say about Susan's relationship with Jake in September 1881 when his father, William, who ran a grocery store in North View, Ludworth, appeared in court facing a charge of committing a breach of the Explosives Act. It appears that Mr Jopling, who sold gunpowder in his store, stored it wrapped loosely in paper in a barrel and that a quantity of loose powder was found lying in the bottom of the barrel when the premises were visited by Superintendent Scott to check its safe storage. In Mr Jopling's defence, he claimed he had received the powder in that state from the manufacturer and felt the breach was down to them and not him. The magistrates sympathised with this point of view but felt it was the shopkeeper's responsibility to complain to the manufacturer about the haphazard way in which the gunpowder was wrapped when delivered. They fined him 1/- plus costs.

Miners had to pay for their own gunpowder for use down the pit and it was available from two outlets within Ludworth – Hall's post office and grocery store and William Jopling's grocery shop. The miners were also responsible for providing their own equipment such as shovels and picks, which were also available at the two stores.

Hannah didn't say anything directly about the incident, but implied that the Joplings were a family 'to be watched'. Susan ignored her mother, realising that anything she said would lead to another argument on the subject. Jake was 27 and Susan 24 by this time and both hoped to marry someday but preferred to do so with Hannah's blessing. However, Susan was running out of hope that this would ever happen.

Hannah often had Lizzie Archer's young son, John Joseph, at her house. He was 6 years old and felt the loss of his mother more than the other children. His older siblings had married and moved out of the village, while the others were not much older than John Joseph. Hannah enjoyed having the young lad around as none of her grandchildren lived in Ludworth. Son Ralph had moved to Sunderland Bridge, Croxdale, during one of the many lay-offs at Ludworth pit and when Hannah went to visit she often took John Joseph with her and he became firm friends with Ralph's son, William, who was 10 years old.

Another shock that rocked Hannah's family in 1881 was the death of her son-in-law, Billy Baldwin, her daughter Ann's husband. Hannah had always liked Billy. She had known him from the days they all lived in Paradise Row and the two families had been a good support for one another. While Hannah was not happy at the way in which his marriage to Ann came about, she still liked Billy and respected him. His father, Neddy, had been widowed in 1870 with the death of Osyth, and Hannah knew he would be devastated at the death of his eldest son. Neddy had remarried in 1873 to the woman who had been working as his housekeeper after Osyth's death.

It turned out that Billy had died of typhlitis, an infection of the bowel that developed after it had been strangulated for three days. Ann had six children ranging in age from 1 to 16 years of age. Her second son, Harry, aged 11, was born with a disability. He had a withered left hand and a club foot. His sister, Sarah, born in 1874, suffered the same affliction and son George, born in 1879, was described as an 'imbecile' on the 1891 census. Harry and Sarah were referred to as a 'cripples' during their childhood, which was the accepted term used at the time.

Hannah had often wondered if these afflictions were anything to do with the first baby Ann lost shortly after its birth in 1865. Ann's second child, Mary Ann, had lived for a year before she too had died of inflammation of the bowel, and these two deaths had put a great strain on Ann and Billy. After Harry's birth, Hannah did wonder whether the baby may have had something similar. Her suspicions were raised even further after Sarah and George were born. Hannah wouldn't know the term, but it appears that Ann's children suffered from some genetic disorder. She didn't say anything to Ann, of course, but felt sure the problems came from Ann's father's side of the family as she didn't know anyone in her family or the Baldwin family who suffered long-term disabilities like the three children. However, as Ann's father was such a secret, and his family were not well known to Hannah, this was a strong possibility.

Hannah travelled over to Trimdon when she heard of Billy's death and stayed with Ann, helping with funeral arrangements and the children until her daughter got herself back into a routine. Ann was able to stay in her colliery house as a result of her eldest son, John, working at Trimdon pit.

Meanwhile, in Ludworth, Susan was continuing to work on the sewing tasks that she and her mother shared and was delighted that with Hannah out of the way she could travel into Durham on a Sunday to meet Jake without her knowing. It was the back end of the year, so the weather wasn't very good, but Susan and Jake had been writing to one another since he moved over to Brandon and they arranged to meet at the statue of the Marquis of Londonderry in Durham market place. They walked around the picturesque riverbanks in the city and up to the cathedral and castle until it was time for them both to make their way back, Susan to Ludworth and Jake to Brandon.

During 1882 Susan became aware of her mother's friendship with Lizzie Archer's widower, Jack. He was a deputy at the pit and, Susan felt, a good few years younger than her mother, but he and Hannah had become friendly over Hannah's interest in his son, John Joseph. Susan was annoyed by this friendship and told Hannah so. 'It's alright for you to have an unsuitable friend, Ma, but you won't let me see Jake when I want to.'

'There's nothing unsuitable about Jack Archer, Susan, so mind your own business.'

'Well I think he is unsuitable,' persisted Susan. 'He's years younger than you and his wife hasn't been dead five minutes.'

'He is a few years younger than me and we're only friends because of the bairn, nowt else. He's not going to ask me to marry him.'

'Well I hope not, because you've stopped me from marrying, and think how unfair it would be if you upped and married Jack Archer.'

'Don't be so daft. I don't know where you get these ideas from,' said Hannah.

The friendship between Hannah and Jack became public knowledge. His older children were as unhappy about it as Susan was, but Hannah wouldn't talk about it. Towards the end of 1883 she told Susan that Jake would be welcome if she wanted to invite him for his tea one Sunday. Jake was back working and living in Ludworth. His father still ran the shop and his grandmother had just died so Jake's aunt, Belle, had taken over the running of the pub. Susan was very surprised at this change of heart. 'Are you sure, Ma? I can't believe you've changed your mind.'

'Well, I see how things are. I realise that if you're going to marry, it's likely going to be to him and I can't stop you now. You're twenty-six and it's about time you settled down.'

Susan couldn't wait to tell Jake. She hoped he didn't turn awkward and refuse to come for his tea. He was very uncomplimentary about Hannah and her rules.

The tea on Sunday went off without a hitch. Jake put on his Sunday best and arrived at the house in Shadforth Terrace as if he'd been visiting for years. Hannah was pleasant, and Susan was amazed that they all seemed to get along. When she said she would walk back to North View with Jake, Hannah didn't object and as they were walking, Susan and Jake talked about how things had taken a sudden change. 'I think it's got something to do with her friendship with Jack Archer,' said Susan, 'but I don't care, at least she's come round at last.'

'Aye and now my grandmother's gone there's no worries about me taking to drink in a big way. Anyway, I'm not messing about any longer,' said Jake. 'Let's get married as soon as we can. I'm nearly thirty years old.'

'Oh Jake, I can't believe it. After all this time waiting for me ma to give her blessing, I just can't believe it.'

'Come on then, let's go and have a drink in the Top House to celebrate,' said Jake.

'Oh no,' said Susan, stopping in her tracks. 'If me ma found out I'd been in there – and on a Sunday – she'd run you out of Ludworth.'

'I know, I was only joking. We can't go taking any chances now that she's come round; we'll do everything we can to keep her happy!'

The news of the wedding was well received by Hannah. She started planning immediately for Susan's outfit and for the food they would need for a small party afterwards, held in Shadforth Terrace. Bill, Jake's father, was also pleased at the news and he said to Hannah when he next saw her in his shop, 'I thought they were never going to get round to it, I can't understand what made them take so long.'

'No, I don't either, they've dithered on for years,' said Hannah.

The couple were married at St Cuthbert's, Shadforth, on 13 March 1884. After the changeable weather at the beginning of the month which consisted of rain, gales, sleet and snow, the weather changed on the 13th to be warm and fine. The couple walked along to Shadforth with their witnesses to the church, which now held such memories for Susan and Jake. Her father and his mother and now his grandparents were buried in the churchyard and they had to walk past all three head-stones to reach the door of the church. The wedding was on a Thursday, which was possible as the pit was idle again. Susan wore a lovely outfit that consisted of skirt, blouse and heavy cape with a velvet hat to match. Jake was in his Sunday best suit and bowler hat.

Once the ceremony was over, they walked back to Ludworth and the family guests arrived at Shadforth Terrace to celebrate the occasion. Ann and her four daughters had walked over from Trimdon, the boys preferring to stay at home, and Ralph with his wife and five children came from their new home at Haswell Moor. In addition, Jake's father, Bill, was there with Jake's brother, John, and his wife, who lived near Hannah in Shadforth Terrace. Hannah's three-tier jam tart created a talking point as it always did, and she served home-made ginger beer for the wedding party.

Susan and Jake moved into their colliery house after the wedding. It was number 15 Cross Row – the single-storey accommodation that Susan had lived in when her da was killed at the pit. They settled in well and Susan saw her mother every day as they were still involved in dressmaking. By September, Susan thought she might be pregnant. She discussed the matter with her mother and they decided as the weeks went on that she was. Jake was over the moon. Susan's sister-in-law, Hannah, was pregnant at the same time. She and Susan's brother, Ralph, were now living in Haswell Moor and Susan would often walk over to visit them when Jake was at work. She could get some practice in with Ralph's children – he had five. Susan would also walk over to Trimdon to see her sister, Ann, who had six children by this time, some of them grown up. The walk to Trimdon became impossible as the pregnancy progressed as it was a long way over the fields from Ludworth. Ann didn't get over to Ludworth much either. Since her father-in-law had remarried she didn't make the effort to visit and left it up to him and his new wife to travel to Trimdon to see the children.

Susan's daughter was born in June 1885 and they called her Rachel after Jake's mother. Bill Jopling was tickled pink: 'Rachel would have loved that little lass – that's all she wanted, and instead she got four lads.'

Looking back, Susan couldn't remember what happened between the birth of Rachel in 1885 and the bombshell announcement her mother made later in the year, when she announced that she was marrying Jack Archer.

'You are what?' cried Susan.

'You heard, I'm getting married and there's nothing you can do about it.'

'Ma, I can't believe you. He's ten years younger than you at least, he's a deputy at the pit. His daughters don't like you. What are you thinking of?'

'Look, Jack's lonely and so am I. We might as well be living in one house where we can keep each other company.'

'But he has at least five of his bairns at home, can they not keep him company or are you going to be their new mother, at your age?'

'Will you stop going on about my age. I'm sixty-four. That's not old these days.'

'Well at least now it's becoming clear why you suddenly gave me the go-ahead to get married, because you had this planned all along didn't you, Ma? I wondered what had brought about your change of heart. You hated Jakey for years and made no secret about it and then all of a sudden it was alright for me to marry him, and all because you were planning this little surprise for us all – Jack Archer included if I'm not mistaken.'

'Now look here miss, I didn't plan anything. He asked me to marry him and I said yes.'

'Well, I'm sorry, Ma. I would like to believe you, you being a big chapel woman, but I just don't. I think you've used me and Jake and I don't want anything to do with you at the moment.'

Hannah and Susan didn't speak after that conversation for a number of weeks. Susan heard that her mother and Jack had married at Usworth Church near Washington. His family were as unhappy about the arrangement as Susan. Ralph, however, was more forgiving, 'Aw Susan, she's old enough to make her own mistakes, leave her be.' Their sister,

Holy Trinity Church, Usworth.

Ann, had a similar view to Ralph, but Susan felt hurt by what she saw as her mother's manipulations over the years that had stood in the way of her relationship with Jake.

Hannah moved into Jack's house in Overman's Row, Ludworth, where she became the mother figure to his children. However, things didn't go smoothly for the newlyweds and by 1891 Hannah had either left Jack or he had put her out; whatever the circumstances surrounding their separation, Hannah moved into private rented accommodation at 5 Margaret Street, Ludworth. This street of private housing had been built in 1885 and was a terrace of twelve houses with two rooms downstairs and three upstairs. By taking on this responsibility, Hannah was once again going against what was expected of a working-class woman. Jack was also living in Ludworth after the breakdown of their marriage. He was living with one of his daughters in Sunniside. It was unheard of for working-class women to leave their husbands, upon whom they were reliant upon for money and accommodation. By marrying

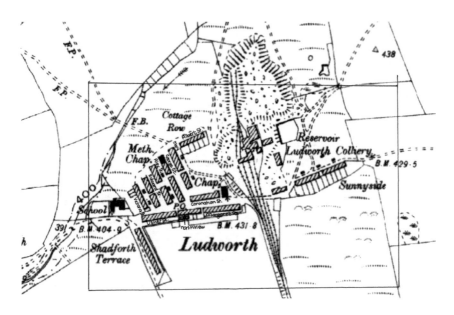

Map of Ludworth, 1890s.

Jack, Hannah had given up the rights to her small pension from the Permanent Relief Fund and to make ends meet and to pay the rent on the Margaret Street property she took in a female and a male lodger.

Throughout her life, Hannah had provided a dressmaking service for people of her own class or those just above it, which suggests that some working-class women were unable or unwilling to make clothing for their own families. However, with the coming of off-the-peg clothing in the 1890s, the skills of a dressmaker who depended wholly on that occupation were redundant. As another way of adding to the family budget, Hannah opened a shop in the front room of the Margaret Street property from which she sold hardware and fancy goods. Her relationship with Susan, who still lived in Ludworth, continued to be distant. They didn't visit one another and barely spoke when they met in the street. However, it was Hannah who Susan turned to after the death of her second child in 1888, a daughter they had called Hannah. The little girl lived for just nineteen hours and Hannah knew better than anyone how it felt to lose a child. The relationship between mother and daughter resumed as they shared the grief of losing the child, but it was not the same as it had been. Hannah was thrilled, however, in June 1891 when Susan gave birth to another daughter, Hannah Jopling.

Hannah's shop in Ludworth was a huge success. She visited Sunderland regularly by train to visit the warehouse that provided the goods to sell. She caught the train from Haswell Plough, chose her items and arranged for them to be delivered later in the week to Ludworth.

In June 1887 Hannah helped provide tea for the villagers as they celebrated Queen Victoria's fiftieth year on the throne. The celebration was held at Tower Farm in a field loaned by Mr Davison. As the pit had been idle for three years and therefore money was tight among the residents of Ludworth, a few local businessmen contributed to the costs of the tea and almost the whole village took part. The Relief Committee, which operated throughout the village during the time of the pit closure, attempted to feed the Ludworth children three times a week, but was totally reliant on gifts of goods or money. However, without such a scheme, many children and their families would be starving. The committee chairman was Douglas Hall from the shop and post office in North View, and he frequently wrote to the *Durham Chronicle* to thank people for their kind donations and in an attempt to attract more contributions.

Unfortunately, Hannah's relationship with Susan did not improve. They were still civil to one another but the closeness they once shared no longer existed. This led to Hannah becoming a regular visitor to her daughter, Ann, and her family in Trimdon. After his marriage in 1890, at least one of Ann's sons, John, her eldest and a deputy at the pit, moved to the Barnsley area to work. He and his wife, Barbara, stayed there for about ten years. There is a family photograph of Barbara and John, who remained childless, with Hannah, taken in an Oldham studio by Squire Knott, a reputable Victorian photographer operating in both Barnsley and Oldham. A child of about 6 or 7 years of age also appears in the photograph but there is no description of who he might be.

Hannah's daughter, Ann, aged 59, married for the second time at St Paul's Church, Deaf Hill, in February 1900. Her new husband was widower Michael Moorin, four years Ann's junior. It doesn't appear that Hannah objected, as she continued to spend time with Ann and

Image of John and Barbara Baldwin with Hannah, late 1890s.

Ann Baldwin, Hannah's first-born daughter.

her family. Perhaps she realised that she couldn't take the moral high ground as a result of her failed marriage to Jack.

Ann's next eldest son, Harry Baldwin, opened a newsagent's shop in Trimdon Colliery during the 1890s and appears to have owned the premises next door in Commercial Street, which he rented out. Hannah

Harry Baldwin's newsagent's shop, Trimdon Colliery.

was staying at Trimdon with Ann in April 1901 when she heard that Susan was pregnant again. 'Well I hope I'm still here to see the bairn,' Hannah said when told the news.

At the time of the 1901 census Hannah was staying at Commercial Street, Trimdon, with Ann and grandson Harry Baldwin, and this is where she was to spend her last days. She died at that property on 19 May 1901. Her death certificate states that she died of senile decay – a term often used to describe old age. Her granddaughter, Mary Ann Baldwin, now married to John Luke, was the informant of her death, indicating that her Trimdon family had become very important to her during the last years of her life. Hannah didn't get to see Susan's youngest daughter, born in January 1902 and named Isabella Jameson Jopling, but there's no doubt that she would have disapproved of the child being given the middle name of someone who once ran a public house!

Hannah was buried in St Cuthbert's Church in Shadforth in the same grave as John Porter and her children. The stone lists the occupants of the grave and at the bottom of the stone the words 'and Hannah his wife' were inserted, as she was the last member of the family to be buried in that plot. There is no visible recognition when looking at the gravestone in Shadforth churchyard that Hannah was 'Archer' at the time of her death, and I believe daughter Susan will have been instrumental in this. The matter of Hannah's second marriage wasn't talked about and its existence died in the memories of her two daughters, never being discussed with future generations.

Susan was responsible for emptying Hannah's house in Margaret Street and incorporated many of her mother's possessions into her own home. One of these was the four-poster bed. Jake couldn't believe it. 'But we'll never get in the parlour bedroom for it, it's far too big.'

'It fits in these cottages and I want to keep it,' said Susan defiantly. 'It just sums me ma up – it's as awkward as can be and can be relied upon to create an argument.' Jake shook his head, realising he was beaten in this particular argument.

One night when she was looking through a biscuit tin where her mother had kept odds and ends, Susan came across Hannah's marriage certificate for her marriage to John Archer. She scrutinised the document and then put it on the table, and with a smile on her face said to herself, 'Well I might have known. She was a strange one, me ma. I wonder if Jack Archer found out how old she was after the wedding?' The marriage certificate stated that Hannah was 61 in 1885 at the time of her second marriage, when she was actually 64 – exactly ten years older than Jack. Susan continued to smile and, shaking her head, she put the documents back in the tin.

AFTERWORD

An analysis of Hannah's experiences shows that living with a coal miner demanded tremendous resources and commitment from a woman. It highlights the poor housing provided by the coal owners and the heroic efforts of women such as Hannah to create attractive, healthy and happy homes in appalling social conditions in order to demonstrate a pride and respectability to the rest of society. Women's work was seen as marginal in mining communities and not considered important.

This was a very unfair assessment of the women who supported coal miners. In Hannah's case, her behaviour and decision-making often went against the social expectations consistent with her class. The first indication of this is when she didn't marry when expecting her first child. She showed a determination at this point in her young life that was probably unique to a girl in her position. This strength of character came to the fore again in 1856 when John Porter went to Australia looking for work and she stayed behind to look after her family. Staying required her to work both on the farm and at her sewing tasks in order to keep a roof over their heads. She gave birth to a child, buried a child, had a child married and moved to a new house while John was away – all major events that she coped with without the support of a husband.

There is no doubt that over the eight or more years John was away, Hannah grew in confidence and in the knowledge that she could support herself and her children without the physical support of a man. She was, of course, receiving financial support from John throughout his time in Australia, but with regard to running a household she developed a very effective decision-making strategy based on confidence and self-belief that would continue throughout the rest of her life. They may not be the decisions expected of her in society at the time but by ignoring the social norms, she did what she thought was best.

Hannah's second marriage is a good example of this. It was an unpopular decision not supported by significant members of their families, but she was determined to go through with it, losing her small pension from the Permanent Relief Fund in the process and causing long-term damage to her relationship with her youngest daughter. When the marriage didn't work out, she had no hesitation in leaving her husband, which was most unusual within the mining community. Most women needed the financial support of a husband to survive and for accommodation and many endured unhappy marriages in order to achieve these two things. Hannah ignored what was expected and took on the responsibility for private rented accommodation, taking in lodgers to help pay the rent and opening up a shop selling hardware and fancy goods from her front room. This was a risky venture in such a small village as Ludworth as goods such as this could be done without; they did not represent the necessities of life, and in fact some were luxuries. However, the shop proved very successful and necessitated Hannah visiting warehouses in Sunderland on a weekly basis to replenish her stocks.

Hannah would never have imagined that someone might write a book about her life, but the more I researched and the more I found out, the more I felt her to be a very worthy candidate of recognition for the part she played in supporting men involved in the Durham coalfield.

I have been unable to find out who the father of Hannah's illegitimate daughter Ann was and while there was much speculation, it is safer to say her father was unknown, as Hannah did on the day of the baptism.

BIBLIOGRAPHY

Books and Articles

Banham, J.D., 'Business Development and Banking in North East England 1755–1839' (Abridged extract from a thesis submitted in partial fulfilment of the requirements of the University of Sunderland for the degree of Doctor of Philosophy), 1997.

Beamish Museum, *The Colliery & Pit Cottages – a Teacher's Guide*, 1994.

Benson, J., *British Coalmining in the Nineteenth Century* (Gill & MacMillan) 1980.

Buddle, J., 'Diaries of John Buddle' (Durham County Records Office).

Burgess, K., *The Origins of British Industrial Relations: The 19th Century Experience* (Croom Helm) 1975.

Burt, Thomas, *Thomas Burt, MP, DCL, Pitman and Privy Councillor* (T. Fisher-Unwin) 1928.

Chadwick, E., *Report on the Sanitary Conditions of the Labouring Population of Great Britain, 1842* (Edinburgh: University Press) 1965.

Church, A.B., *The History of the British Coal Industry – Volume 3 1830–1913, Victorian Pre-Eminence* (Clarendon Press) 1986.

Colls, R., *The Pitmen of the Northern Coalfield* (Manchester: University Press) 1987.

Cooper, P. & Rowland, A.J., *Environment and Health* (Edward Arnold) 1983.

Cronje, E., eds Woods, R. & Woodward, J., *Urban Disease and Mortality in 19th Century England* (London: Batsford) 1947.

Davidoff, Leonora, *The Family Story: Blood, Contract and Intimacy 1830–1960* (Longman) 1998.

Dowding, W., eds Norris, P., *Demographic & Social Change in the Durham Coalfield* (University of Durham) 1986.

Fordyce, W., *The History & Antiquities of the County Palatine of Durham* (T. Allan) 1850.

Fowler, Lucinda, *Marriage, Mining and Community in 5 Durham Parishes* (MA thesis, University of Durham) 1984.

Fynes, R., *History of Northumberland and Durham Miners* (Thomas Summerbell) 1873.

Hair, P.E.H., *The Social History of British Coal Miners 1800–1845* (unpublished thesis).

Hall, Catherine, *Private Persons versus Public Someones: Class, Gender and Politics in England 1750–1850 in White, Male and Middle Class* (Cambridge, Polity Press) 1992.

Harris, Beth, *The Works of Women are Symbolic: The Victorian Seamstress in the 1840s* (PhD Dissertation, City University of New York) 1997.

Henriques, U.R.Q., *Before the Welfare State* (Longman: London) 1978.

Jones, C., ed. Sturgess, R.W., *Experiences of a Strike: The North East Coalowners and the Pitmen 1831–1832 Essays in Coalmining in the 19th Century*, 1986.

Lawson, Jack, *Peter Lee* (Hodder & Stoughton) 1936.

Lawson, Jack, *A Man's Life* (University of London Press Ltd) 1951.

Leifchild, J.R., *Our Coal and Our Coal Pits* (Frank Cass & Co.) 1868.

Levine, Philippa, *Victorian Feminism 1850–1900* (University Press) 1994.

Levine-Clark, Marjorie, *Engendering Relief: Women, Ablebodiedness and the New Poor Law in Early Victorian England* (Journal of Women's History 11.4) 2000.

MacFarlane, A., *Modes of Reproduction in England 1300–1840* (Blackwell) 1986.

Moore, R., *Pitmen, Preachers and Politics* (Cambridge University Press) 1974.

Perkins, Joan, *Victorian Women* (Murray) 1993.

Redmayne, R.A.S., *Men, Mines and Memories* (Eyre & Spottiswood) 1942.

Rymmer, Edward A. ed. Neville, R.G., 'The Martyrdom of the Mine or a 60 Years Struggle for Life' (History Workshop) 1 spring 1976 and 2 autumn 1976.

Shadforth History Group, *Shadforth – A Village History* (Shadforth History Group) 2006.

Shoemaker, R., *Gender in English Society 1650–1850* (Longman) 1998.

Thomas, R.L., *The Eclectic Practice of Medicine* (Scudder Brothers, Ohio) 1907.

Thompson, D., *Outsiders: Class, Gender and Nation* (Verso) 1993.

Vicinus, Martha (ed.) *Suffer and be Still: Women in the Victorian Age* (Methuen) 1980.

Wheatley Hill History Club, *The Thornley Coal Company, Owners of Thornley, Ludworth and Wheatley Hill Collieries 1830–1885* (Wheatley Hill History Club) 2002.

Wheatley Hill History Club, *The Weardale Steel, Coal & Coke Company, Owners of Thornley, Ludworth and Wheatley Hill Collieries 1886–1913* (Wheatley Hill History Club) 2004.

Whellan, William, *History, Topography & Directory of the County Palatine of Durham* (Manchester: Galt) 1856.

Wilson, John, *Memories of a Labour Leader* (T. Fisher Unwin) 1910.

Newspapers

The Durham Advertiser
The Durham Chronicle
(Durham County Records Office)

Newcastle Weekly Chronicle
Northern Liberator
(Newcastle Central Library)

Northern Star
(Tyne and Wear Archives)

Sunderland Echo
(Sunderland Local Studies Centre)

The Times
(timesonline.co.uk)

Maps and Plans

Plan of Miner's Cottages
Plan of Paradise Cottages
Drawing inc. Margaret Street, Ludworth
(Durham County Record Office)

Durham County Council Geographical Information System (GIS) –
Historical Maps